The Christ Centered Prayer

The Christ Centered Prayer

Revelation – The Strait Gate and Narrow Way

Reverend Sandra Casey-Martus, MEd, MTS
Carla Mancari, MEd, Spiritual Guide

The Christ Centered Prayer: Revelation – The Straight Gate and Narrow Way

Published by Wheatmark®
1760 East River Road, Suite 145
Tucson, Arizona 85718 USA
www.wheatmark.com

ISBN: 978-1-62787-349-9 (paperback)
ISBN: 978-1-62787-350-5 (ebook)
LCCN: 2016931705

. . . behold,
the Kingdom of God
is within you (Luke 17:21).

The contents of this book are not meant to take the place of qualified medical professionals or therapists. The authors give no expressed or implied guarantee as to the effects of the suggestions, and they assume no liability. The authors' realizations, revelations, and testimonials in this book are true.

Contents

Acknowledgments

WE ARE THANKFUL to all of you who have wholeheartedly embraced the Christ Centered Prayer. We are pleased with the feedback you have shared depicting the positive life changes the prayer has had in your lives.

Beverly Ann Randolph is always willing to give a helping hand. Her comments and suggestions were useful.

We appreciate Mary Carpenter (Christ Centered Prayer and yoga teacher) for sharing her insights. I am blessed that the Reverend Sandra Casey-Martus (coauthor, teacher, and devoted disciple of Jesus Christ) for not only sharing her spiritual journey but also patiently editing a difficult manuscript. Her diligent effort helped clarify a complex work.

We are grateful to the Right Reverend Bishop John S. Thornton for the foreword. He is a blessed friend who generously contributed his thoughtfulness and time.

With the deepest love, we honor Jesus Christ and His Holy Spirit for the gift and revelation of the Christ Centered Prayer method.

Foreword

I KNOW SANDY AND Carla. I've known them a long time. I know them well, gratefully. I've assisted Sandy and Carla at retreats in Idaho, Arkansas, and Texas. They have made a difference in my life as a Christian just from my having watched and listened to them. They will do the same for you.

Working independently and collaboratively, Carla in Florida and Sandy in Texas, by every means of communication and during retreats, they are now sharing half a lifetime of experience and reflection in a settled, unarguable, quiet conviction. And let me tell you this: with that settled, unarguable, quiet conviction, you will find nothing tentative or timid about them. Sandy and Carla are not afraid to engage the world as it is, not as they wish it were.

Finally, I have a suggestion. Read chapter 4 first. That chapter contains a description of the Christ Centered Prayer practice. Then practice the method. Once you have done that for a while, everything else in the book will make perfect sense. As you read the book—perhaps two or three times—enjoy especially, as I did, those wonderful short, pithy, wisdom-laden sentences, such as, "We're the cross that the Christ calls us to bear."

May you daily—twice daily—be collected by the Christ. So that your life will be such that all the world may come within the reach of the saving embrace of Jesus Christ.

The Rt. Rev. John S. Thornton, Bishop of Idaho (retired)
April 2015[1]

1 Printed with letter of permission.

Preface

In 1973, while visiting a shrine in Lourdes, France, I had my first mystical experience. I had been working at the time as a certified counseling psychologist, but afterward, I resigned and began a spiritual quest. I traveled the world, studying with Christian, Buddhist, and Hindu masters. My spiritual truth seeking ultimately brought me into a relationship with Jesus Christ. This relationship allowed Jesus to reveal the Christ Centered Prayer method via the straight gate and narrow way.

I met Reverend Sandra Casey-Martus at a retreat center in 1993. We formed a teacher-student relationship. I worked with Sandy until she was firmly grounded in spiritual truth and a relationship with Jesus Christ.

Sandy and I founded the Contemplative Invitation Teaching, and Sandy began to share the Christ Centered Prayer method. The response to Christ Centered Prayer has always been phenomenal. It has changed lives, and with it, many have been brought into the reality of a relationship with Jesus Christ.

Our book *The Lessons*[1] is an introduction to the Christ Centered Prayer method. It is a study guide of spiritual principles and defines more than two hundred topic lessons that seekers may encounter along a spiritual journey. *The Christ Centered Prayer – Revelation: The Strait Gate and Narrow Way* is an informational, all-inclusive inventory of the profound possibilities of truth. It provides rich details of how Christ Centered Prayer will assist you in turning within. Its purpose is to help those who wish to understand the Christ Centered Prayer method, its workings within the Spiritual Heart Center, and its profound power to assist you in realizing the awareness of the Holy Spirit in the name of Jesus Christ.

Your kingdom is not of this world. Your peace beyond understanding is not of this world. Your eternal life is not of this world. The awakening to your kingdom, peace, and eternal life are within.

In *The Christ Centered Prayer – Revelation: The Strait Gate and Narrow Way*, our intention is to make known a sacred, silent prayer revealed for this generation and for the edification of all future generations. Christ Centered Prayer supports, strengthens, and deepens an ongoing relationship with Jesus Christ through the power of His Holy Spirit. "For through him we both have access by one spirit unto the Father" (Eph. 2:18).

Truth is full of contradictions. We must use the word *you* throughout this book to communicate on this relative plane

---

1 Sandra Casey-Martus and Carla Mancari, The Lessons: How to Understand Spiritual Principles, Spiritual Activities, and Rising Emotions, Volume One (Tucson: Wheatmark, 2008).

of opposites. In reality, to realize truth is to go beyond the personal sense of a *you*, realizing truth is true freedom.

Scripture verses are from the Holy Bible, King James Version, London: Syndics of Cambridge University Press, Bentley House, American Branch, New York, printed in Great Britain.

Respectfully,
Carla Mancari, Coauthor

One

What Do You Want?

Longing

In seeking and finding,
Truth is revealed.
In silence and secret,
longing is healed.
– cm

WHAT DO YOU want? What is it you seek? What do you long for? Why are you reading this book? How did you hear about it? Did someone give it to you? Were you simply curious? Whatever your answer is, you did not just happen to come by this book. You are responding to an inner invitation.

You are ready for what follows because "there is a longing within you that instills a belief that there is more. A longing that never lets you forget that there is something beyond the appearances of this world. It is a longing within you that creeps into your awareness at unexpected moments of solitude."[1]

This longing is not in your mind. The longing is an itch that cannot be scratched. The deeper the itch, the greater the restlessness as the mind twists and turns. Your spirit will find rest only when you discover that for which you are longing.

You may be under the false assumption that only mystics, ascetics, or ordained religious individuals receive the call to realize the intimacy and oneness of God in this life. This is simply not so. God extends the invitation to holiness to all people, here and now.

As history attests, traditional church leaders who desired a more moderate pursuit of the spiritual life for themselves and their constituents ended up thwarting many ardent truth seekers. To squash the fervor of genuine seekers is as disastrous to the church as adopting an attitude of anything goes. A prudent respect for scripture, reason, experience,

1 Carla R. Mancari, *A Diet for the Soul: The Minute Method* (Bloomington: WestBow Press, 2011), 32.

tradition, openness to the present, and the yet-to-be realized initiatives of the Holy Spirit provide all of the necessary checks and balances.

Yes, religious passion is powerful and challenges the structures of religious institutions even as it breathes life into them. It is a delicate discernment for you, as a Christian, to undertake and not shy away from that for which you are longing. Draw aside the mind's curtain that would obscure and deny your access to the greater dimension of your reality.

Reverend Sandy, during her early ministry, was without a prepared sermon; her total dependence was on the Lord's presence. She stood before her congregation and revealed that for which she had longed for her entire life:

> Trinity Sunday asks preachers to articulate a doctrine promulgated in 325 AD at the Council of Nicea, and read it back into the scriptural texts provided for the day. It is the only Sunday that celebrates the doctrine, in this instance, that of God as One in Three Divine Persons: Father, Son, and Holy Spirit—the Trinity, as it is commonly referred to.
>
> The Trinity is perhaps the quintessential mystery of Christian faith.... I found myself in a quandary, unable to find any inspiration whatsoever for the sermon. As each day passed, I thought, *Surely tomorrow will bring some clever new insight or story*. These never appeared.

As the congregation sat down, I stood perfectly still, feet firmly planted on the wooden floor for balance, and in utter silence. My mind was a total blank. I stood for what seemed to me like an eternity. I was unaware that tears were welling up in my eyes and starting to literally drip down on my alb. I continued to wait on the Lord, and a thought came from deep, deep in my heart.

I said slowly and through the tears, "All that I know is that in my life I have longed in the deepest part of my heart for that which I cannot understand, for that which I cannot find words for because the longing comes not from my head but from the silence of my heart. "I have spent my entire life in hot pursuit of that mystery. And what I can say to you today is only this: that mystery for which I have so deeply longed for has more deeply longed for me."

Again, I paused, and at this point, I was aware of the tears and the tinge of embarrassment at what I might say next. I concluded, "My message to you is, long for that which you cannot know in your head, cannot write on a piece of paper, has no name, no form, but can only love. Then take that mystery, which longs for you and for me; embody it; enact it; and give it to every person, plant, and animal on the planet. In that way, you shall know God."

The sermon ended in the same silence in which it began. I turned around with tears of gratitude.

> Not only had I preached, but also, more importantly, I had received a message and a teaching. I know for a certainty that mystery I had so deeply longed for, longed even more deeply for me. My life, my heart, my head, and my preaching have since never been the same.[2]

The depth of Reverend Sandy's heartfelt longing brought her into the Lord's presence. Her preaching and her life had changed. Reverend Sandy's lifelong pursuit was met in a moment of the realization that her longing was reciprocal.

There is an inner nagging that will eventually turn you in the direction to seek that for which *you* long. No one and nothing can give it to you or take it from you. You must realize that you are an individual expression of God's love.

Become renewed through the Christ Centered Prayer method. You have been longing for this. You are reading *The Christ Centered Prayer – Revelation: The Strait Gate and Narrow Way* because this is what you want!

---

2 Sandra Casey-Martus and Carla Mancari, *The Lessons: How to Understand Spiritual Principles, Spiritual Activities, and Rising Emotions, Volume One* (Tucson: Wheatmark, 2008), 124–125.

Two

The Spiritual Heart Center

Your "Other Heart"

I sought you, Lord, in all of the
noise of this world, in every part.
I sought you, Lord, until…
I found you in the silence of
my heart.
– cm

WITHIN YOUR BREAST is a subtle vibrating energy. It is a spiritual vibrating energy center within your physical form (at the center of the chest, between the breasts). We refer to it as the Spiritual Heart Center, the heart of God, or your "other heart" (because of its proximity to the physical heart).

The Christ Centered Prayer method addresses a subject rarely discussed by Christians: the Spiritual Heart Center. Christians often ignore the Spiritual Heart Center's availability and access.

Why the Spiritual Heart Center? It is the innermost sanctuary of your being. It is the Holy of Holies that is so near, and yet individuals may easily overlook it. It is where the teachings of the Holy Spirit in the name of Jesus Christ emanate.

Within the Spiritual Heart Center, the Holy Spirit in the name of Jesus is an active, vibrating energy force. The Holy Spirit is the ultimate teacher. It pours forth and reveals truth for your understanding. All too often Christians tend to forget in whose name the Holy Spirit is sent. "But the Comforter, which is the Holy Ghost, whom the Father will send in my name, he shall teach you all things, and bring all things to your remembrance, whatsoever I have said unto you" (John 14:26).

Exactly where is the access to the Spiritual Heart Center? "It is not a mystery, nor is it difficult to find. There is never a time when the Holy Spirit in the name of Jesus is not available. 'Neither pray I for these alone, but for them also which shall believe on me through their word; that they all may be one; as thou Father, art in me, and I in thee, that they also may be one in us: that the world may believe that thou hast sent me'" (John 17:20–21).[1]

When you practice the Christ Centered Prayer (chapter 4), you may access the Spiritual Heart Center within you and connect with the Holy Spirit in the name of Jesus Christ. Revelations and realizations are born here. The vibrating energy is invulnerable power. It may dissipate sorrowful remorse, soothe a troubled heart, and restore your relationship with Jesus Christ. It is here where you rest in the shadow of the Almighty. "He that dwelleth in the secret place of the most High shall abide under the shadow of the Almighty" (Ps. 91:1).

You may tend to shy away from that which you are not familiar. Venturing beyond the known into the depths of your Spiritual Heart Center may require courage. Traveling the inner path may be a challenge. The idea of seeking the unknown can be frightening. You may prefer to stay with what you know rather than risk the unknown.

An old story goes something like this: after God created humankind, He called to one of His angels and asked the angel to hide the one thing He wished to conceal:

> "I have finished except for one thing, the mystery of life. Where shall you hide it?" God asked the angel.

---

1 Sandra Casey-Martus and Carla Mancari, *Your "Other Heart": The Best-Kept Secret* (Tucson: Wheatmark, 2010), 99.

"I will hide it in outer space," responded the excited angel.

"No," said God, "man one day will easily find it there."

"All right, I will hide it on the moon. Surely it will not be found there?"

"No, no," said God, "one day he will be able to look there also. Mmm," thought God. "I have it! Put it within him. He would never think to look there."

For Christians the heart is a symbol of the Sacred Heart of Jesus. The Sacred Heart of Jesus Christ continuously touches your heart in the oneness of His love. It is a love that guides you to the awareness of your reality.

A particular Christian recognition of the Holy Trinity points to your Spiritual Heart Center. You may be among the many Christians who learned the sign of the cross at an early age but gave it little significance. You honor and express your belief in the Holy Trinity whenever you make the sign of the cross and say, "In the name of the Father [center of forehead], and of the Son [center of chest], and of the Holy Spirit. Amen [shoulder to shoulder]."

Making the sign of the cross has *great* significance. When you do so, you point directly to your Spiritual Heart Center. Look in a mirror while making the sign of the cross. Notice that the upper part of your body has the appearance of a cross. You are the cross you are asked to take up to follow Jesus. "And he that taketh not his cross, and followeth after me, is not worthy of me" (Matt. 10:38).

The Spiritual Heart Center is right under your fingertips. Every time you touch the center chest area and say, "And of the Son," you are pointing to your Spiritual Heart Center. You need look no further. You have found it. The Christ Centered Prayer practice mimics the sign of the cross. It, too, goes directly from your head to your Spiritual Heart Center, your "other heart."

The Spiritual Heart Center is a powerful, vibrating energy. Your life's direction may change when you become aware of it. You may find the joy of the spiritual path there. You may realize that you are not alone. You may find that the truth of your inheritance is as a beloved child of the Most High.

The indwelling light of the Spirit of God beckons you to seek and enter into the Spiritual Heart Center. The darkness of this world cannot comprehend the light that radiates within you. This light's radiant warmth comforts and holds you in the center of the heart of God, your Spiritual Heart Center.

Christ Centered Prayer softly guides you to your Spiritual Heart Center, where you may access the Holy Spirit in Jesus's name. The ultimate work of the Holy Spirit in the name of Jesus is to transform you through divine love. In reality yours is a giving God nature that gives eternally in infinite variety. The gifts of mercy, love, and forgiveness reflect the nature of God. These gifts are your birthright. You may realize them within your Spiritual Heart Center.

This world knows nothing of the Holy Trinity of your being. It cannot begin to comprehend the things of your godly nature. This world can only marvel in wonderment at a divinity it knows not. All the strength and action you could ever desire in your life exist in every vibration of your Spiritual Heart Center.

Enter through the door of your inner sanctuary. Become aware of the presence of Jesus Christ. Do not deny yourself that which is yours by divine birthright, your oneness in the presence of Jesus Christ.

You may become aware of the following:

» Forgiveness and purification
» The still, small voice in silence
» An inner world of spiritual reality
» The realization of the Christ of your being
» The doorway to the eternal God being is accessed
» The outer world as a reflection of the inner world
» The Holy Spirit in the name of Jesus Christ revealing truth
» Your inner master, Jesus Christ, who guides and holds you in the light of divine love
» The oneness of God's essence, Jesus's Holy Spirit, inviting you to wake up to your reality

The Holy Spirit within your Spiritual Heart Center may accomplish all of the above and infinitely more. Your heart, soul, and mind, devoted to the love of God, will guide your footsteps into an expanded vibrating Spiritual Heart Center. "Jesus said unto him, Thou shalt love the Lord thy God with all thy heart, and with all thy soul, and with all thy mind" (Matt. 22:37).

Within your Spiritual Heart Center, through the Holy

Spirit in the name of Jesus Christ, all mystical mysteries are resolved. Here, all realizations and wisdom rise. It is here that you may realize your uniqueness—the "Word" made flesh. "For in him we live, and move, and have our being; as certain also of your own poets have said, For we are also his offspring" (Acts 17:28).

Reverend Sandy struggled with the meaning of life until she was guided to the Holy Spirit in the name of Jesus Christ within her Spiritual Heart Center. She found an understanding and peace of mind there:

> Under stress I find myself questioning and contemplating the "meaning of life" issues. As I gaze about, I get the gnawing feelings of disillusionment and entertain thoughts like "What's the use? It's all a sham. Why bother?" Temptations and attractions rise, enticing me to value the things of this world as being more deserving of my attention than my relationship with Christ.
>
> I have a sense of my nothingness in the midst of nothing. All the work and messing around on this planet, for what? A grand mental construct? Everything just seems such a sham and I wonder why I continue to be concerned and what the fuss is all about. I feel like no one, nowhere, doing nothing, and someone somewhere doing something all at the same time. What difference in the

> big scheme of things does it make? What difference do I make, if any?
>
> The mind's tricks and temptations certainly suggest doubts, fears, and criticisms until I again realize, value, and appreciate the Christ of my being. Only then does my mind go to the edge of the universe and look back on the cosmos with a sigh. Then the wonder of the Christ within my open heart stirs.[2]

Reverend Sandy overcame her temptations, doubts, and fears. The overcoming brought her to the realized presence of the Christ.

Christ Centered Prayer takes you directly into the powerhouse within you, your Spiritual Heart Center. It is an Almighty God powerhouse of energizing, illuminating, and vibrating energy. Nothing is untouched by it. It steadies your balance between the appearance of two different worlds—the inner and the outer. It is within this powerhouse that you may realize the kingdom of God.

All are invited to become aware of this powerhouse of possibilities that work through you, with you, and as you. In the powerhouse of your Spiritual Heart Center, the Christ of your being carries you through the shadows of doubts, desires, and temptations of this world.

---

2 Sandra Casey-Martus and Carla Mancari, *Your Other Heart: The Best-Kept Secret* (Tucson, AZ: Wheatmark, 2010), 135–136.

Powerhouse of Possibilities:

» Opens minds and soften hearts.
» Reveals the infinity of your reality.
» Seeks you where you are in the present.
» Guides you back to before birth and after death.
» May heal tormented emotions and broken hearts.
» May bring you into alignment with the will of God.
» Is where truth, justice, love, and reconciliation reside.
» Covers you with the warmth of compassion beyond this world.
» Opens the door to the power that created the universe and sustains it.
» Reveals the power inherent in the forgiveness-purification process.
» Touches your soul and turns you inward toward the kingdom of God—your kingdom.
» Assures you of your well-being and self-esteem in the abiding surety of God's presence.

In the Christ of your being, as a child of God, the law of God is written in your heart and governs the inner workings of your being. Go where the action is, where the powerhouse of possibilities are, realize life everlasting, and that which facilitates an awareness of inner silence. This silence is readily available to you. When you are drawn to seek truth, your inner silence deepens. Tuning into the silence away from the chatter of this world and its concerns is important. With an awareness of your Spiritual Heart Center, you may hear the silence and discover that your needs are provided for in such a way that you may accomplish whatever is necessary, including making decisions.

The Spiritual Heart Center allows darkness to be dispelled and the light of awareness within you to be revealed. Leave your sorrow behind. Realize that you are not alone. Trust that Jesus delivers on His promise: "And ye now therefore have sorrow: but I will see you again, and your heart shall rejoice, and your joy no man taketh from you" (John 16:22).

The Spiritual Heart Center reveals endless truth in infinite variety and expression. The purpose of the Christ Centered Prayer method is to guide you to the awareness of your Spiritual Heart Center area where, in the Christ presence, your reality is realized. No gift is greater.

Numerous references to the heart appear throughout the Bible and Christian literature (appendix). The Holy Scriptures contain a road map to the door of Jesus's presence, His Holy Spirit. Look in the least expected place for the mystery of life: within *your* Spiritual Heart Center. Here is where your heart and soul will bask in the awareness of the Christ.

No code is necessary to become aware of your Spiritual Heart Center; no secret password, introduction, or referral is necessary. Your entrance is assured. It is up to you to become aware of it. It is always within *you*. Go for it!

Just knowing *about* God will never be enough. You will always have that longing to realize God, to realize the divine will of God. The Christ Centered Prayer method is the vessel that carries you across the river into your Spiritual Heart Center. Get in, and take the ride of your life—which may take you to the end of the beginning of your life.

Three

The Christ Centered Prayer Method

Revelation

A revelation!
The pearl of great price.
A gift to this generation.
–cm

THE CHRIST CENTERED Prayer method is a silent, contemplative prayer practice that Jesus Christ revealed. He had insisted, "Teach them the Christ Centered Prayer and be assured, this generation is ready to receive it." The Christ Centered Prayer method is offered as a means to access your Spiritual Heart Center easily so that you may establish, through the power of the Holy Spirit in the name of Jesus Christ, your relationship with the risen Lord. It is a simple method to learn. It acknowledges and builds upon all previous contemplative teaching, tradition, and biblical reference.

What makes the Christ Centered Prayer method the pearl of great price, the Holy Grail of silent prayer methods? It is a revelation—the straight gate and narrow way to the Holy Spirit in the name of Jesus Christ. The Christ Centered Prayer method is a unique contribution to the inner journey. It is the direct path to your inner life with Jesus Christ and beyond.

The Christ Centered Prayer method encompasses all of the various realizations (chapter 10-11). The Christ Centered Prayer method is all about an inner journey to the realized awakened state of being.

The Christ Centered Prayer method's simplicity is both its difficulty and its strength. Its greatest difficulty is that it *is* an easy practice. You will encounter no complicated instructions with rigid rules and demanding postures. Individuals are accustomed to meditation prayer methods that require a measure of difficulty, and as a result, easy becomes difficult. To be so easy and yet so profound in its ability to reveal truth is also its strength. It can only leave you in awe!

As an authentic private revelation, the Christ Centered Prayer method does not contradict any previously revealed, publicly accepted truth. It may also deepen, broaden, and clarify previously accepted revealed truth. The validity of any private revelation is always measured against the sense of the faithful and builds up the community of faith even as it may edify the recipient.

A prudent respect for tradition and an openness to the present and the yet-to-be realized initiatives of the Holy Spirit in the name of Jesus Christ provide the necessary checks and balances. The two are never mutually exclusive.

All silent prayers have their value, but they have differences among them. The Christ Centered Prayer method cuts to the chase. It allows nothing to stand between you and the reality of your God being through the power of the Holy Spirit in the name of Jesus Christ.

You may be firmly established in truth. Rooted and grounded in love, your silent prayer method and your life are built upon hallowed ground. "That Christ may dwell in your hearts by faith; that ye, being rooted and grounded in love, May be able to comprehend with all saints what is the breadth, and length, and height; And to know the love of Christ, which passeth knowledge, that ye might be filled with all the fullness of God" (Eph. 3:17–19).

Infinite power and profound rest grace the Christ Centered Prayer method. It is a subtle, calm inner prayer method that allows you to move effortlessly into the awareness of your reality. Here you may identify with your God source.

The Christ Centered Prayer method is not in competition with other contemplative prayer methods. The Christ Centered Prayer method has a delightful and relative ease about it. It drops familiar traditional aids, such as a sacred word, thought, image, sound, or breath, as it articulates a simplification of the ancient traditions.

The Christ Centered Prayer method does not separate your inner practice from your outer practical living. When you practice it with determined purpose, the fruits of love, joy, peace, goodness, kindness, meekness, gentleness, patience, and self-control may express themselves naturally in your daily life. As individual expressions of divine love, these fruits testify to God's purifying, loving, and healing presence.

This Christian contemplative prayer method facilitates a posture of alert receptivity and cultivates a deep silence. It becomes an inner peace. Within this peace, you may awaken to your oneness. The less background chatter, the more inner silence. Yes, less *is* more.

Once you have the courage to turn within and live with the quiet silence, you discover it is your nature. The inner and the outer merge in a calm, peaceful environment. The silence allows the awareness of the Christ to express its presence naturally. Living with constant background noise and chatter of your home environment obscures the quiet silence.

Reverend Sandy thought that I was asking too much of her to live in a quiet home environment for even a short while. After an intense struggle, she was willing to do it:

This is a lesson I really resisted. I thought after having given up my caffeine drinks that would be enough for a while. I was forever not wanting to stay home alone. I would find a hundred and one things to do away from the house. Don't get me wrong. I loved my home and enjoyed being in it but had to have the background chatter of television going on. Especially in the morning.

It was my habit to come downstairs for my morning toast and a cup of decaf coffee. And, of course, the first thing I did was to turn on the TV.

My teacher had been, for some time, trying to get me to experience the delight of a morning of quiet silence. Often, she would say, "If you would allow yourself to experience the quiet silence within yourself, the less the chatter of this world will bother you and the more time you will have."

This, I thought, was going a bit too far. Surely a little television wasn't going to hurt me. No, it would not hurt me, but what I was not realizing was that it was depriving me of the enjoyment of realizing the quiet silence within when I was in a silent prayer period and when I was not.

So, what the heck! It was Lent, and I thought why not give up the television time for Lent. So, I did. And, yes, it made a difference. It did take a little getting used to. At first, it seemed strange. I would get home and have dinner. It was so different without the television. I thought, *I have never done this before.* I ate and was more aware of my food. I enjoyed the stillness and the quiet. I looked around and thought, *Well, what do I do now?*

My teacher was right. There was more time. I sent an email to my teacher and said, "No television gives lots of time. I am enjoying it?" Then a strange thing happened. A few days later, I was at a conference. I glanced down at the *New York Times* headlines a friend was reading, and I asked, "What is this shooting about?"

He looked at me in utter dismay. "You mean you haven't heard about it?"

Then I remembered of course not. I have not turned the television on for several days, and, no, I had not heard. He thought I was out of my mind. What I decided was that I was better in my right mind for not having been poisoned in the early-morning hours by the horrible story. It was interesting.

Lent season was a good excuse for Reverend Sandy to experiment with a quiet home environment. She was pleasantly surprised to find that a quiet home environment did have its benefits. It taught her that the returns were greater than what she had given up.

Making a change from your normal routine can be a challenge. You have been conditioned "to do," and sometimes "overdo," to get what you want. You push, shove, and drive yourself to the brink to get what it is you believe you want.

It is always a getting and holding on. Effort, effort...all is effort.

Now you are instructed to do the opposite of what you have been taught. No pushing, no shoving, no holding on, and no driving yourself anywhere. The greatest effort is to show up, practice the Christ Centered Prayer a few minutes twice daily, and be patient. Your journey is unique to you.

The mind takes you on an outer journey. The attraction of appearances and false concepts govern its destination. The Christ Centered Prayer method takes you on an inner journey to the aware reality of your being.

Jesus went beyond the traditions and the teachings of His day. Jesus revealed through His example and teaching that you, too, can go beyond the traditions of your day. Jesus never condemned traditional teachings. He fulfilled the law while revealing life eternal. His was a kingdom not of this world. The Christ Centered Prayer method may slowly, carefully, and lovingly restore the remembrance of that kingdom.

The God that is known by faith dwells within you always. The Christ Centered Prayer method is for those who have an interest in responding to God without mental or verbal words and in solitude, simplicity, and silence. Jesus guides you through His Holy Spirit to your God reality. "Jesus saith unto him, I am the way, the truth, and the life: no man cometh unto the Father, but by me" (John 14:6).

The Christ Centered Prayer method may guide to where truth, which had been hidden for all ages, is revealed. It points you beyond words and images. Once the value of the method is appreciated, you may take joy in a practice that gifts your life with an aware presence of Jesus.

This world fears what it does not understand or cannot destroy. This world believed it could destroy and put to death Jesus's teaching of salvation and freedom. It could not. It did not. The awareness of your being is just *be-ing* without definition—nothing more, nothing less. "And God said unto Moses, I AM that I AM" (Ex. 3:14).

You tend to identify with that which has been created and conditioned (a false self) rather than realize you are creation *itself*, the reality from which all is manifested. The following comments are from Christ Centered Prayer method participants. They tell how the Christ Centered Prayer method worked for them.

Comments:

» "The presence of my Lord is realized.
» "I sleep better, and my health has improved."
» "My children tell me I'm easier to get along with."
» "I am more balanced and stable in everything I do."
» "I am more flexible when things don't go my way."
» "I am less prone to anger and to harboring resentments."
» "It is a life-changing event. The silence is profound."
» I experience more joy in my life and self-acceptance."
» "I am happier, and my friends say, 'You're nicer to be around.'"
» "I have more clarity and discernment in my business decisions."

» "My life seems to unfold with less stress, more clarity, and greater ease."
» "My emotional responses to life's ups and downs are more appropriate and less exaggerated."

In coming home to the reality of their being at the deepest level, the participants report an ability to remember what their lives are all about. By faithfully practicing the Christ Centered Prayer method, folks report that they return to their daily activities with renewed energy and a refreshed sense of purpose. The comment most often made is, "It changed my life." Such reports are indeed an incentive for you to practice the Christ Centered Prayer method and reap its benefits.

The Christ Centered Prayer method may keep you centered, balanced, and at peace during transitional times. It is your shelter during the storm and your resting place during the calm. Through it, you may rest in the awareness of the presence of the Christ of your being.

The Christ Centered Prayer method fulfills Jesus's invitation to "come and find rest for your souls." With Jesus as model, scriptures as reference, tradition as custodian, sacraments as celebration, and selfless service as mission, the Christ Centered Prayer method draws its source, sustenance, and direction.

This method guides quietly and efficiently to realize all that you are and always have been. The Christ Centered Prayer method promises nothing, and yet it may deliver all. It is for you to take advantage of a Christian prayer method that thoroughly and painstakingly carries you to the awakened state beyond an illusionary world.

Telling you a Spiritual Heart Center exists is not enough. Telling you about the Christ Centered Prayer method is not enough. Telling you to turn within is not enough. Telling you where to turn within is not enough. Telling you about participants' comments is not enough. You need to know *how* to turn within to access your Spiritual Heart Center. The Christ Centered Prayer practice *is* the *how*.

Four

The Practice

Three Easy Steps

Come down off your perch.
The time has come …
begin an inner search.
– cm

As a follower of Jesus Christ, you may take the "strait gate and narrow way" to the recognition and acceptance of Jesus Christ as your guide and master. The Christ Centered Prayer practice carefully responds to Jesus's invitation to "follow me," and it painstakingly leads you on a spiritual journey to your all-inclusive God presence.

The Christ Centered Prayer practice articulates a simplification of ancient tradition. The practice does not require any aids because in reality, *you* are the sacred *word*, the *Word* that existed in the beginning. "In the beginning was the Word, and the Word was with God, and the Word was God. The same was in the beginning with God. All things were made by him; and without him was not any thing made that was made" (John 1:1–3).

Reverend Sandy writes of the value of a contemplative prayer practice in her life. She notes why, in comparison with other silent prayer practices, the Christ Centered Prayer practice holds sway in her life:

> This has not been a quick journey, and I am still en route. The one thread that has held me together has been fidelity to a practice of contemplative prayer.
>
> During my forty-plus years of uninterrupted silent prayer practice, I have found that my inner practice has moved in the direction of less and less effort and more and more awareness. The delightful and relative ease of the Christ Centered

> Prayer practice, compared to other prayer practices, holds sway in my life.
>
> Through direct invitation and guidance of the Holy Spirit, whom we know supersedes all methods, we are gently led to an awareness of the risen Christ who dwells in our innermost Spiritual Heart Center. Access to the Divine Indwelling is not only possible, but practical. Inspired and encouraged by this, I find the silent Christ Centered Prayer practice may assist us in the realization of the Divine Indwelling. It is the Divine Indwelling awareness that the Christ Centered Prayer intends.[1]

It was the ease of the Christ Centered Prayer practice that initially attracted Reverend Sandy. However, it was the realization of the "risen Christ" that convinced her that the Christ Centered Prayer practice could help others in the awareness of their reality.

The practice is simple and easy. You will find no time prescribed rituals and no use of words, thoughts, sounds, images, or breath. The Christ Centered Prayer invites you to rest in the "Word" and silence of who you are in the awareness of your Spiritual Heart Center area. "And the Word was made flesh, and dwelt among us (and we beheld his

---

1 Sandra Casey-Martus and Carla Mancari, *The Lessons: How to Understand Spiritual Principles, Spiritual Activities, and Rising Emotions, Volume One* (Tucson: Wheatmark, 2008), 22–23.

glory, the glory as of the only begotten of the Father), full of grace and truth" (John 1:14).

Christ Centered Prayer Practice:

1. **Sit comfortably, close your eyes, inhale a long deep breath, and exhale slowly. Relaxing your entire body, continue to breathe normally.**
2. **Consciously become aware of your Spiritual Heart Center area (center of chest, between the breasts) and rest in awareness.**
3. **When thoughts or sensations rise, do not dialogue, converse, engage, or respond. Again, become aware of your Spiritual Heart Center area, and rest in awareness.**

Is that not easy? You do not need to complicate the Christ Centered Prayer practice. Easy *does* work. The practice takes you directly to your Spiritual Heart Center area. However, *you* must do the practice.

Hearing, touching, seeing, tasting, and smelling—these are impressions received through the physical-body organs of perception. These sense impressions and thinking may draw your immediate attention. Again, become aware of your Spiritual Heart Center area and rest in awareness.

Practice the silent Christ Centered Prayer at any time before a meal and at least two hours after a meal (the changing energy vibration will interfere with the digestion process). Begin the prayer for a few minutes, and allow it to extend itself naturally over time. There is no prescribed length of time required.

At the end of a prayer period, open your eyes, move your hands and move your feet. Before returning to your normal activities, take a moment to become consciously aware of your mental and physical senses as they rise.

Remember, you are not trying to make anything happen. You are not seeking to *feel* anything. The mind feels. You are resting in awareness of your Spiritual Heart Center area beyond the mind and body states of consciousness.

Be consistent, and practice the Christ Centered Prayer twice a day. When sitting on a chair, you may wish to sit on one with arms for support. Sitting on a cushion on the floor and using a prayer shawl are also options. If for any reason you find it difficult to become aware of the Spiritual Heart Center area, place your hand upon the Spiritual Heart Center area for the first few prayer periods.

You may already have formed the habit of practicing a different prayer method. An established habit is not always easy to discontinue immediately, especially if it is one of long standing. A habit is an act of interest often repeated. Replacing one prayer practice with another need not be difficult.

If a previous prayer practice rises to compete with your new practice, do not get upset. To struggle only reinforces the old habit. With loving kindness, allow the old established prayer practice to rise, and treat it as you would any other thought. Do not dialogue, and again become aware of your Spiritual Heart Center area and rest in awareness. Gradually, the old practice will no longer rise.

Change of a prayer practice is a natural progression on your spiritual walk. Jesus Christ has been waiting for you.

He will lovingly welcome the change. Enter effortlessly, silently, and directly into the recognition of the fullness of your God nature. Inherent in His glory is the realization of the oneness of your reality. What is true of Jesus is true of you. "And the glory which thou gavest me I have given them; that they may be one, even as we are one" (John 17:22).

You cannot separate yourself from the Word that was in the beginning and was made flesh. The Word was made flesh, and it remains the Word of God. The Word of God is eternal truth. "Of his own will begat he us with the word of truth, that we should be a kind of first fruits of his creatures" (James 1:18).

Be faithful, patient, and disciplined in the Christ Centered Prayer practice. It is not wise or useful to judge or evaluate your practice based on your experiences during the prayer. The fruit of the prayer is always realized in daily life, as the Holy Spirit in the name of Jesus Christ insinuates itself spontaneously. "But the fruit of the Spirit is love, joy, peace, longsuffering, gentleness, goodness, faith, meekness, temperance: against such there is no law" (Gal. 5:22–23).

The Christ Centered Prayer practice facilitates your participation in the divine word, which you are. Without extraneous dialogue, stringent guidelines, or complicated definitions, the Christ Centered Prayer practice bypasses potential distractions that the mind loves to create.

In addition to practicing the Christ Centered Prayer twice a day, you are encouraged, if possible, to attend a Christ Centered Prayer retreat. Energy vibrates at different frequencies; therefore, sit with individuals who are practicing the Christ Centered Prayer method. You will find your practice is easier and supported when like-minded individuals sit together.

Mary Carpenter, Christ Centered Prayer and yoga teacher, shared her retreat experience with Reverend Sandy and Carla. She has come to fully appreciate teaching, practicing the Christ Centered Prayer, and attending a retreat:

> I have a greater awareness of how powerful the Christ Centered Prayer is in people's lives. It is palpable to me that each person was affected by the retreat and that each got exactly what they needed from the retreat. I felt the presence of the Holy Spirit guiding me.
>
> I am so solidly clear that the quality of the prayer experience is insignificant. It does not matter if I have a monkey mind or slip into deep quiet, because the fruits come in my daily living.
>
> My meditations before the retreat, and frankly most of the time anyway, are constant thoughts with constant returning to the awareness of my Spiritual Heart Center area. What I learned during the retreat was that there is a great desire in me to purify my thoughts and doubts.
>
> I guess I had been doubting if my prayer practice was "good enough," because my mind was so busy. I now can see how effective the Christ Centered Prayer is. Yes the prayer has helped me much these past few years.

> I know these words don't give justice to the powerful impressions made upon me at the retreat, but I know I have been deeply changed. Thank you both for sharing the Christ Centered Prayer with me.[2]

Mary discovered that a Christ Centered Prayer retreat made a difference in her life, and in the lives of others. Her life would never be the same.

If you sit with others in a group session, you need not sit longer than twenty minutes. If you are a new member and find twenty minutes too long, you may easily take breaks by opening your eyes and then begin the prayer practice again at comfortable intervals. Do not be concerned about the size of a group. One in the Christ is a majority. Just get started, and others may join when they are ready. "For where two or three gather in my name, there am I in the midst of them" (Matt. 18:20).

The Christ Centered Prayer practice may easily and effortlessly open your Spiritual Heart Center directly to the awareness of the Divine Presence within. Through direct invitation and guidance of the Holy Spirit, you are softly led to an awareness of the risen Lord.

There are times when you may become discouraged with your Christ Centered Prayer practice. You may question if you are progressing as well as others. It is a natural occurrence for you to drift occasionally into a previous traveled

2 Printed with a letter of permission.

mind state of consciousness. A drift may cause you to become lax with your spiritual practices.

There is no un-manifested consciousness. Whatever has been impressed upon your consciousness will manifest. You may, for a time, suppress or repress events, thoughts, and memories; however, given a moment of space, all will eventually rise.

You are always working on yourself. The Christ Centered Prayer practice progresses you on your spiritual journey. Second-guessing what is going on with other individuals during a Christ Centered Prayer practice is unnecessary and counterproductive. Keep watch over your own practice. "Watch therefore: for ye know not what hour your Lord doth come" (Matt. 24:42).

Jesus is with you every step of the way. He is with you through your fears, your ups, and your downs. Be assured, your spiritual journey *is* His priority. Jesus does not give one moment and take away the next. No, Jesus does not play like that. "LORD, thou hast been our dwelling place in all generations" (Ps. 90:1).

Jesus will not love you less because of a drift. All that you have realized is not lost. Whatever has been realized, although it may fade for a time, will rise again. Jesus is not with you until death do you part, but for life eternal. As Jesus is in the Father, you are in Jesus, and Jesus is in you. You need only realize it. "At that day ye shall know that I am in my Father, and ye in me, and I in you" (John 14:20).

You may discover that your inner and outer lives share much in common. In reality, all life is spiritual activity. Whether washing dishes, scrubbing floors, or sitting in silent prayer, you may come to do all things with conscious awareness. Your inner guidance is seamless. You may come to be as aware of God's abiding presence in your practical living as you are during your silent prayer practice.

As you practice the Christ Centered Prayer, you may discover that the mind finds a way to distract you from becoming aware of your Spiritual Heart Center. The mind is an expert at creating obstacles during a silent prayer practice.

Practice with a determined purpose. Doing so will help you overcome the mind's favorite obstacles. A determined purpose is the willingness to invest your time and energy to do the practice a few minutes twice a day. The greatest value of having a determined purpose is the focus and guidance it may provide.

The Christ Centered Prayer practice may turn obstacles into stepping stones that lead to the blessed peace within. The following are a few of the obstacles, during a Christ Centered Prayer practice, in which the mind may revel. Your awareness of them may shorten their life span.

1. Alone and Lonely

You may feel discomfort with the idea of being alone because you think of it as being lonely. Both have in common the inner message *one* (al*one* and l*one*ly). Alone rests in the One. Lonely seeks the One. This world has so many tempting attractions after which to chase. You may, at times, do anything not to stay home alone.

When you are attached to a separate sense of a personal self, you experience a separate existence. You experience a sense of being lonely. Loneliness seeks a deeper presence of your nature, the oneness.

Alone and lonely are no longer obstacles once you are no longer drawn to the background noise and chatter in your home environment. When you live with the quiet, you may come closer to realizing your true nature. The inner and the outer merge in a calm, peaceful environment, an environment where loneliness does not exists and being alone is restful, not restless.

2. *Attention*

Attention is your interest instantly alerted by the rising of thoughts, senses, or sense impressions (acting as stimuli) within your consciousness. The state of an object of interest holding your attention is called attentive concentration. Attention becomes an obstacle when it attaches you to a thought, emotion, or sense impression.

Attention is the mind's most devious obstacle. It is the easiest for the mind to use during a silent prayer practice. Your attention is immediately attracted to whatever appears within your conscious mind. As your attention is attracted, it may seem to have a will of its own.

You subject yourself to suffering, pain, or pleasure by attending to or attaching emotions to the conditioned sense impressions or rising thoughts. It is your attracted interest that holds your attention. The greater the attraction, the greater chance that attention may become an obstacle.

Thoughts and sense impressions do serve a purpose on this plane, when not practicing a silent prayer. They allow a conscious flexible exploration of rising thoughts and sensations that may contribute to creativity, ideas, or resolutions.

As you continue the Christ Centered Prayer practice, the attention obstacle may gradually decrease. You may have a greater awareness of your spiritual nature. You have a choice over which thoughts and sensations you engage, act upon, or let go. You are in charge. This is interior freedom.

3. Complacency

You may become satisfied with your realized spiritual unfoldment. Complacency becomes an obstacle when you have lulled yourself into the false belief that you have surrendered enough. It is when your spiritual progress is at its smoothest that your boat may rock and the complacency temptation will rise. Understanding why your boat should be rocked during what appears as smooth sailing may be difficult.

Complacency often invites a resistant stiff-necked response to any inner or outer nudge to take another step on the straight and narrow path. The Christ Centered Prayer practice takes you beyond into turbulent deep waters. A struggle with a temptation actually has the capacity to make you stronger and more convicted.

Yours is a spiritual nature with many facets. The willingness to embrace the difficulties of yet another unknown facet of your spiritual nature allows a realized transition to be a more welcomed one.

4. *Inflexibility*

You may want to sit for your first practice of the day in the morning and your second during the afternoon or evening. If you find getting in a daily second practice is difficult because you cannot find the time due to work, errands, children, and a million other things on your agenda, it is understandable. Any change in your daily routine may become an obstacle that may be met with resistance.

All too often, you may be attached to a particular time or place for your practice. You want everything to be exactly the same. This may be ideal, but it is not always practical. An active lifestyle may require flexibility at any time. Flexibility with your Christ Centered Prayer practice gives you the freedom to adjust to new routines.

Be flexible. Restrooms are everywhere, aren't they? You go to the bathroom sometime during your busy day, don't you? So use one for a minute. It is that easy. John can be very helpful. In fact, "John" may become your best friend.

5. *Greener Pastures*

You may be one who believes the grass is greener just beyond your own practice. It is difficult to remain faithful to your Christ Centered Prayer practice and progress if you have only one eye on where you are and the other on seeking greener pastures.

In this world, greener pastures may appear one day and fade the next. Where you are is where the grass is the greenest. If other pastures tempt you to them, the grass will be just as green, no greener.

This is a world of many pastures. You could easily wander aimlessly from one pasture to the next. The greener pasture that you seek is the one you are standing in and with the maintenance of the Christ Centered Prayer, the greener *it* becomes. The green pastures do not change. You do. The brilliance is within you. Stay with your Christ Centered Prayer practice.

6. *Internal Dialogue*

In the Christ Centered Prayer practice, internal dialogue is a conditioned response to rising thoughts or sense impressions (hearing, touch, sight, taste, and smell). It is the busy work of the mind. Internal dialogue is an obstacle that produces no benefit. It sidetracks and stalls a silent prayer practice.

When your attention is attracted to rising thoughts, emotions, or senses, an internal dialogue may begin. Dialoguing is an obstacle that interferes with the immediacy of consciously returning to the awareness of your Spiritual Heart Center area. Dialoguing negates awareness of the present moment of silence; any spiritual realizations of your God-given nature will be overshadowed and slip beneath the radar.

Internal dialogue deals primarily with past memories or future expectations (planning). Neither memories of the past nor expectations of the future exist in the present. When a past memory rises with an attached emotion (positive or negative), dialoguing recreates the event as if it were happening in the present. Such indulgence serves no useful purpose. Not dialoguing with rising thoughts or memories is important.

If you do *not* dialogue with rising thoughts, emotions, sensations, and images, they will *not* become obstacles—

they will simply fade. Not dialoguing with the rising attractions of this world, in or out of a prayer practice, allows you to "be still, and know that I am God" (Ps. 46:10).

7. *Mixing*

It is important to remember that you are working with individual expressions of consciousness. A chosen path has a particular state of consciousness, be it the Buddha, Allah, Krishna, or the Christ. You should always practice your prayer with individuals who support your chosen path's state of consciousness and to mix is an obstacle to your progress.

To believe or insist that it does not matter will not change the spiritual principle of like consciousness. If you insist on continuing to mix and explore, you are creating an obstacle to finding your way by the straight gate and narrow way. Your Christ Centered Prayer practice is not a social event. The Christ Centered Prayer is a sacred, silent prayer practice. Treat it as such.

The Christ Centered Prayer practice establishes you in the presence of Jesus's unconditional, nonjudgmental love emanating within the Christ consciousness—your consciousness. You do not need to get upset with any obstacle or whatever rises within your consciousness. Just renew your priority and continue your prayer practice.

As you progress on your chosen path, it is your responsibility to guard and protect each state of consciousness you have realized. The straight and narrow way is just that—straight and narrow. Creating obstacles and detours only delays the awakening to the reality you are seeking. "Strive to enter in at the strait gate: for many, I say unto you, will seek to enter in, and shall not be able" (Luke 13:24).

You are always working on yourself. It is your inner journey. Your every thought, word, and deed has a ripple effect. Whether you are near or far from the consciousness of other individuals, the ripple effect of your thoughts, words, and deeds may have a positive or negative influence.

An act of kindness—or an unkind act—multiplies. Be aware if you think one thing but say another. Your thoughts, as well as your spoken words, vibrate and go forth. Be faithful with your Christ Centered Prayer practice, and keep your actions gentle. Think twice before you speak and three times before you act. What you send out by spoken word or thought will surely return to sender.

When you open your eyes and get up from your cushion, your prayer does not end. The flow of your life should be seamless twenty-four-seven. There is no time when you are other than a spiritual being. The interior freedom to engage (or not) continues in your daily activities.

Expect a pause here and there along the way. Jesus understands, and although at times the awareness of His presence seems to fade, it is only your awareness that has dulled, *not* Jesus's presence. You are not starting over, beginning again, nor going backward. You are continuing.

Practice is the key. Sit for a few minutes twice a day, and rest in the awareness of your Spiritual Heart Center area again and again. Like the prodigal son, you are returning to your Father's house (chapter 16). Jesus awaits your return. With patience, you will find that Christ Centered Prayer has a life of its own. Relax, enjoy, and let the prayer *do* you. This is the *how*.

Five

Forgiveness, Purification, and the Holy Instant

Interior Cleansing

Bruised from head to toe,
forgiveness, purification, the holy instant …
restores white as snow.
– cm

QUESTIONS MAY RISE: "What exactly is happening when I do the Christ Centered Prayer practice? What is going on when I do not dialogue and again become aware of my Spiritual Heart Center area?" The possibilities of insights, realizations, forgiveness, purification, and the holy instant are what is going on. All of which may lead to an awareness of the reality of your being.

The Christ Centered Prayer practice facilitates the process of forgiveness, purification, and the holy instant. As a result of this process, you come to an understanding of truth teaching with the least amount of time and effort. "Let this mind be in you, which was also in Christ Jesus" (Phil. 2:5).

As you sojourn through this world of life and death (chapter 17), you may have misused (polluted) the purest of your energy through thought, word, or deed. This misuse of your individualized energy must be restored to its original state. It is your responsibility to restore it. You may do this with the Christ Centered Prayer practice through the power of the Holy Spirit in the name of Jesus Christ.

Forgiveness and Purification

Forgiveness and purification are the gradual cleansing of the distortions and misuse of your energy. The Christ Centered Prayer practice is a turning consciously inward, becoming aware of your Spiritual Heart Center area, and resting in awareness. As you do this, the forgiveness-purification process intensifies. This intensification allows your vibrating energy to be restored to its original state.

It has been said, "I will forgive but never forget." You

cannot talk about the forgiving part without talking about the not forgetting part. True forgiveness is forgetting (letting go). It does not mean you will no longer remember. Your memory remains intact, but the suffering attached to the memory's event no longer exists.

The process of forgiveness and purification covers yourself and everyone who may come to mind. It is the gift of your nature that may be given freely and cause no harm. The prefix *for* translates to "away, apart, off." One of the definitions of *give* is to inflict punishment. So to forgive is to do away with, not to inflict punishment.

As you come into compliance with your God awareness, you may experience an unexpected release of tears of joy. You may find you seek silence, tend to speak less, and listen more. That may be a good thing! Forgiveness and purification are a necessary beginning for the mystery of life to be revealed.

Benefits of Forgiveness and Purification:

» Softens the spiritual journey.
» Allows the holy instant to occur.
» Quickens the purification process.
» Allows the reconciliation experience.
» Covers a multitude of sins (ignorance).
» Opens the inner door where silence pervades.
» Is the unconditional love for yourself and others.
» May progress you to higher states consciousness.
» Frees the necessary energy for a more productive, practical life.

Reverend Sandy struggled with her concept of forgiveness. Even though Jesus was quick to forgive, she wanted forgiveness on her terms:

> Maundy Thursday I went to sleep and had an experience of encounter with Jesus, my Risen Lord that was vivid, lucid, audible, and etched in my consciousness. I do not know exactly how long this encounter lasted, but I do know that it took as long as was necessary for me to get the point of the visit. Jesus wanted me to know the essence of reconciliation, divine union.
>
> When I emerged from the experience, I wrote it verbatim. To this day, I have never changed a word of it. The following is the verbatim. I will later offer reflections.
>
> Clothed in brilliant white, face unseen yet known. Tall in splendor knowing, He says to me, "Come home."
>
> From deep within His being, He gently beckons me, "Let go of all your sorrows. Come in me and find your 'peace.'"
>
> "One moment, Lord." I close my eyes, I need to go within. A second to reflect, I thought, before I can begin. Time then stopped in stillness. How long I cannot say.
>
> Lost somewhere within His love my Lord in me did pray.
>
> "What of our encounter, Lord? You know we never had our chat."

"Hush, my child. Be still. Can you see? It's over just like that."

"But Lord, it was too easy, to forget myself in thee. I wanted to tell you all there was. But you only wanted me."

Jesus simply appeared to me in full radiance and filled my entire conscious awareness. The brightness of the light was indescribable. Jesus's invitation and gesture to come home was explicit.

When everything stopped, the only language I can use to describe this time is utter stillness, nothingness, void. This was a long "nothing," and only after returning to awareness and again conscious of Jesus's presence did I know I had been lost somewhere, although I had no knowledge or memory of where I had been or how long. The fact was Jesus had pulled me into Himself and beyond the radiance of Himself into a place I had no earthly knowledge of nor ability to understand until fairly recently.

Whatever did go on in that gap prepared me for the culmination of our encounter. Initially fully to realize the full impact of the gap, I resumed the conversation, trying to remind Jesus that I had not even mentioned my litany of sins.

The conversation was personal, direct, and respectful. To my astonishment, as in the biblical story of the Prodigal Son, there was absolutely no interest on Jesus's part to hear any of my stories. Rising to the occasion, of course, I told Him to wait a minute so I could get myself in order before I began my rehearsed litany of sins.

Jesus was not about to entertain that litany nor was He interested in the past. I will never forget Jesus's look of amazement when He simply responded,

"Hush, my child. Be Still. Don't you see, it's over just like that."

The humor was lost on me at the moment and continues on to this day. It seems to be my nature not to be able to leave well enough alone. I continued:

"No, no, Lord that is not the way it is intended to be. It's supposed to be hard, humiliating, and embarrassing."

I suppose I was going to give Jesus a lesson on how to hear a confession! It was at that moment of remonstration that I finally understood. Ah! I get it. I wanted to tell Jesus all there was. However, Jesus was only interested in me, and Jesus only wanted all of me!

The split second that realization dawned in my consciousness, Jesus disappeared. Not one second sooner or later. The moment I had the realization of true forgiveness—to put away punishment—and experienced reconciliation, then at-one-ment, a complete sense of peace and light, filed my entire being. My true nature was not separate from God but deeply one in God through Christ. Amen!

Now years later, I realize the infinite patience

> and tolerance my Lord had for my dramas. I also know that there comes a time when He draws the curtain! I know what is true for me is true for all. It is for this reason that I share this little story.
>
> It profoundly illumined my mind and healed my heart. Forgiveness truly means to do away with or put off punishment. Jesus was not interested in my mistakes, but He was keenly interested in my well-being and in having all of me. In the same way, Jesus saw health and wholeness beneath all appearances and apparent distortions of my human brokenness. He saw Sandy as beloved holy, and restored her to wholeness. Just like that!
>
> To be invited, loved, acknowledged, and drawn into intimacy and union with Christ by the power of the Holy Spirit is a powerful experience of reconciliation. We simply have to be willing to go there and, having been in that embrace, give gratitude and thanksgiving to God who in Christ is reconciling us and the world and everyone in the world to Himself.[1]

Sandy wanted forgiveness and reconciliation, but she found it difficult to accept how easy it was. Jesus Christ did not require her to jump through hoops of any kind. Forgiveness was always available. Sandy wanted it, and she received it. An embrace of grace engulfed her with a sense of well-being.

---

1 Ibid., 156–157.

The forgiveness-purification process is like a soft warm blanket that covers everything and gives you a joyful spirit. A most beautiful peace occurs, a pliable peace that penetrates your entire being in all that you are and do. Forgiveness is the necessary ingredient in the process of purification and the holy instant. It is a natural, limitless gift of your spiritual, divine nature. Forgiveness is the index finger of God touching your soul.

The Holy Instant

It is during the Christ Centered Prayer practice of forgiveness and purification that the holy instant may occur. The holy instant severs the attachment that causes suffering from cause and effect (chapter 17). By attaching a highly charged emotion (hate, anger, or fear) to a hurtful memory, you suffer. A holy instant is a profound instant from detachment of an emotional hurtful memory.

Each time you dialogue with a hurtful memory, you multiply your suffering. A holy instant may do away with an entire history of accumulated hurts. When practicing the Christ Centered Prayer, and you do *not* respond to a rising hurtful memory and *immediately* return to rest in the awareness of your Spiritual Heart Center area, the suffering may cease. A holy instant has occurred.

Benefits of a Holy Instant:

- » Frees up energy.
- » Heals harmful memories.
- » Removes the suffering caused by attachment.
- » Eliminates responses to a rising memory, image, or sound.
- » Detaches painful emotions from rising thoughts, images, or sounds
- » Ultimately dissolves the hold that the habitual cycle of cause and effect has on your awakening to your eternal life.

A holy instant cannot be felt or emotionally experienced. Feeling is of the mind; a holy instant is beyond the mind. What *is* realized is the result. Your memory remains intact. It is the attachment that no longer exists.

You know detachment has taken place (during a Christ Centered Prayer Practice) in a holy instant when the same hurtful memory rises again and you no longer are affected. You are free! Yes, to forgive *is* divine, and a holy instant is an instant of your divinity.

Six

Awareness-Consciousness

What You Are Made Of

Awareness turns off the night.
The one who lights your candle
is the light.
– cm

AWARENESS-CONSCIOUSNESS, WHAT YOU are made of. Although consciousness and its contents vibrate in the light of awareness, you cannot be cognizant of awareness. You can be aware of being conscious, but you cannot be conscious of awareness.

Awareness

Awareness cannot be grasped with the mind. To attempt to understand the awareness reality of your being with the conscious mind is an exercise in futility. The mind cannot grasp that which is beyond it.

Awareness is calm, silent, subtle, and changeless. All states of consciousness are present in awareness. Awareness has no edges. Nothing or no one is ever lost in the universe.

When watching a movie, you are only conscious of the contents appearing on the screen. The screen is the field of awareness. The content is the appearance. You are conscious of the appearance. This is the way awareness exists. It allows the appearance of an image and its contents that are constantly changing, while it, the screen, remains unchanged.

Look out of a window. What do you see? You may see mountains, trees, houses, or animals. Where are they appearing? All appear in the light of day. The light of day is the one thing you take for granted and never consider. You don't say, "Ah! What a beautiful morning in the light of day." You don't say, "Ah! What a beautiful view of the mountains in the light of day." The light is not given any thought. Your attention is on the images, not that which allows the images to appear.

You can never fall out of awareness, nor can you be

conscious of awareness. There is no *I* in awareness, no self-reflection, no self-identity. In awareness, there are no opposites, no separate false sense of a personal being.

It is awareness that makes all states of consciousness and its contents possible. All rise in the light of awareness, the changeless.

Consciousness

There are three layers of consciousness that rise in awareness. We refer to them as spiritual, psychological, and physical. Many *states* of consciousness exist within these three layers of consciousness.

With the Christ Centered Prayer practice, you may realize the three layers of consciousness and their many states. You descend (incarnate) into this world through the layers: spiritual, psychological, and physical.

The return way is in reverse: from the extreme outermost perception to the most inner depth of your Expansive Awareness of be-ing. One way perceived out, and one way perceived back; from the one to the many, from the many to the one. The Christ Centered Prayer practice, straight gate and narrow way, is your spiritual journey in awareness to your reality.

You cannot skip any major layer. All serve a purpose. The mistake that is easily made is for you to get hung up in any one layer and its many states. This prevents your progress. Jesus knows exactly where you are and prepares for you where you may belong. "In my Father's house are many mansions: if it were not so, I would have told you. I go to prepare a place for you" (John 14:2).

An illusion is an illusion no matter in what layer or state of consciousness it appears. However, it has its own reality that is relative to that state of consciousness.

The Three Layers of Consciousness:

1. The Physical-Body Consciousness Layer

The physical conscious layer is the grossest layer and the most familiar. It is the obsessed attachment to a physical body that is a drag on a spiritual walk. Being attached to the personal physical sense of a body keeps you in body consciousness until you progress beyond it.

"Therefore I say unto you, Take no thought for your life, what ye shall eat, or what ye shall drink; nor yet for your body, what ye shall put on. Is not the life more than meat, and the body than raiment?" (Matt. 6:25).

You should respect and care for your body and meet its needs, but you should not worship it. It is what is within you that is sacred. Keep your body in top condition, and it will serve you well as the temple of God. "Know ye not that ye are the temple of God, and that the Spirit of God dwelleth in you?" (Cor. 3:16).

2. The Psychological-Mind Consciousness Layer

The psychological layer is also easy to become attached to and linger in for a long time. This layer, with its different states of consciousness, may contain the possibility of bliss, visions, fortune telling, and manipulative mental powers of the physical sense layer. Any of these manifestations may be difficult to move beyond. The mind's imagination will conjure up all the powers and principalities that are entertaining and often ego inflating.

There are prayer practices that are grounded in scientific or psychological models. It is not necessary for you to bog yourself down with scientific or psychological theories. All the scientific and psychological knowledge you learn on this plane is relative to this plane.

Intellectual knowledge is useful in specific related fields. To apply mental effort to a silent prayer practice is to prolong your spiritual walk. The silent Christ Centered Prayer practice is a direct path to the awareness of the Spiritual Heart Center area and the Christ consciousness. You will be unlearning as you go beyond the physical and psychological layers to the reality of your being.

3. The Spiritual (Christ Consciousness) Layer

Infinite individual expressions of consciousness exist within the spiritual layer. One is yours. You are an individual expression of the one Christ consciousness, never separate nor apart. Your individual state of consciousness changes as you progress on your spiritual journey.

The spiritual layer, Christ consciousness, and its many states may not be any easier to go beyond than the states of mind and body consciousness. The spiritual layer (Christ consciousness) and its many states may express Jesus, the Blessed Mother, saints, and loved ones. These appearances may hold your attention and interest longer than necessary.

The Christ Centered Prayer practice does not ask you to

give up the spiritual, Christ consciousness, layer. You are passing through it as your state of consciousness changes. How long you stay in any of the states of consciousness depends on the attachments you form while in these states. You do not have to stay in any of the states longer than necessary. The reality of your being is beyond the three layers.

With the Christ Centered Prayer practice, you may realize the Christ consciousness. With this realization, a sense of separation ceases. "That they all may be one; as thou, Father, art in me, and I in thee, that they also may be one in us: that the world may believe that thou hast sent me" (John 17:21).

Because of a false sense of being separate—rather than an individualized expression of the Christ consciousness—other individual expressions may become difficult to understand. Ignorance of the oneness causes a lack of communication, manifested evils, and wars on this plane of opposites. Therefore, without a realized Christ consciousness, you may spend a great deal of time and effort attempting to understand and adjust to the various individual expressions of consciousness.

When seeking to realize the awareness of the Christ consciousness, you accept, allow, and respect all manifesting individual expressions of consciousness, as you would your own. "And the second is like unto it, Thou shalt love thy neighbor as thyself" (Matt. 22:39).

You are constantly changing and experiencing different states of consciousness. Individual conscious mind personalities have the ability for change and progress. Consciousness is not set in concrete. All that the conscious mind creates will deteriorate and die. That which cannot last is not real. That which you *are* is permanent; it is real. "Thou fool, that which thou sowest is not quickened, except it die" (1 Cor. 15:36).

Claim your inherent, spiritual right. You are beloved of God and called into being. You are the Word spoken into life from all eternity. What greater testimony to God's infinite love for you is there? You are you, not someone else. In the entire cosmos, there is no other like you. "I will praise thee; for I am fearfully and wonderfully made: marvelous are thy works; and that my soul knoweth right well" (Ps. 139:14).

In truth, you are recognized as the Divine's own. The Lord knows you in all your most finite ways. "O LORD, thou hast searched me, and known me. Thou Knowest my down sitting and mine uprising, thou understandest my thought afar off. Thou compassest my path and my lying down, and art acquainted with all my ways. For there is not a word in my tongue, but, lo, O LORD, thou knowest it altogether" (Ps. 139:1–4).

Letting go of a personal separate sense of *I* results in an awareness of God being oneness. True identity on this plane is God seeing, God hearing, God touching, God smelling, God tasting, and God loving. You are the hands and feet of God in this place. When you smile upon others, you are His face.

Seven

Mind's Contents

Recognition

Ups and downs.
Steady as you go…
through sights and sounds.
__cm

WITHIN AWARENESS-CONSCIOUSNESS THERE are many different forms of contents (thoughts, feelings, and emotions) that rise. In or out of the Christ Centered Prayer practice, you may encounter any or all of them. The attachment of an emotion to a thought or sensation may be so quick it goes unnoticed. Before you are aware, you may be caught up in it. Attachment is the cause of suffering. This chapter, with the Christ Centered Prayer practice, may help you identify and work with the contents.

Contents may rise in no particular order. They rise according to an individual's conditioning, disposition, personal history, experiences, and expectations. A review of the various contents may help you recognize them. You have the power to maintain an alert state of consciousness.

Contents:

1. Anticipations and Expectations

Anticipations or expectations exist in the future. To focus on a possible result demands a constant looking forward. To anticipate or expect either a good result (praise) or a dreaded result (blame) is to anticipate the illusionary world of opposites as your reality. Do not cling to anticipated or expected results. Be fully and consciously aware of a thought at its birth moment.

Live every present moment as though you were in the presence of Jesus Christ. Do as He would do in thought, word, and deed. The presence of the spirit of Jesus Christ may penetrate every pore of your existence.

2. Desert Places

It is when you least expect it that you may find yourself in the desert places. These times may be difficult because they seem to happen when you are most faithful to your prayer practice. What you may not realize is that it is your fidelity that leads you to the desert places during your greatest vulnerability.

You are most vulnerable when you have had a realization or a reasonable time of general "good feelings." The desert places are quick to take hold, inviting desires, doubts, and temptations to rise.

The Christ never abandons you. Do not abandon the Christ. The desert places are a time for attaining greater inner strength necessary to overcome the difficulties in daily life. Continue the Christ Centered Prayer practice twice a day during your dark nights as well as the bright days. Jesus's willingness to confront the temptations in the desert and overcome them prepared Him to begin His public ministry. The same is true for you.

3. Drama

At times, truth may feel like you have been struck with a bolt of lightning, leaving you twisting and turning in a storm. Drama may easily pull you in. Remnants of attachment may be slow to fade, leaving you in fits of temper, anger, and confusion.

Enter the mind player. The mind (mental) states of consciousness can create drama with every possible conflicting thought, impression, or argument to reject the real for the world stage. The mind prefers drama to the "peace beyond understanding."

Drama is a natural result of a mind that cannot comprehend what is going on. It does not want to lose the old you and is fighting hard to hold on to the dream. Trust that the Christ of your being will bring you through to the other side of the dream. "Therefore if any man *be* in Christ, *he is* a new creature: old things are passed away; behold, all things are become new" (2 Cor. 5:17).

4. Anger

Anger is an emotion experienced as hostile feelings. Anger is not a bad or good emotion. It is an emotion that can be put to good use. The anger emotion will rise whenever a need for it exists, but it does not have to cause heartburn, figuratively or literally. To use anger constructively has enormous potential and power to right a wrong or correct an injustice.

You never want to repress anger. Allow yourself to experience it in a safe, productive way. Admit that "I am angry about such and such or so and so. I am so angry I could scream." If you are someplace where you can scream, do it. If not, take a couple of long, deep breaths and use the hand-to-heart prayer practice (chapter 15). Then when you are able—and choose to—express forgiveness and decide the necessary action. Notice the emotion as it rises. Decide how best to express it.

You are not a doormat. Take whatever action is necessary to protect yourself from those who would do you harm.

Do not respond to the anger of others (including yourself for getting angry). This only serves to compound it. Act from a forgiving heart no matter what action you take.

Your intention within the action is what matters. The appearance of anger may be negative, but the intention in its expression need not be. Anger may contain the seeds of forgiveness. That is what dissipates anger and allows you to move on in a productive manner. Here's an example: Your teenager has wrecked the car. You are angry and prescribe punishment; however, within the prescribed punishment is your complete forgiveness, and you are thankful to God no one was hurt. You move on—and so can your child—without harboring ill will.

The best blessing from your work with anger is that as the Christ Centered Prayer (or hand-to-heart) practice dissipates anger, you come to realize the freedom from the letting go of the anger. It is a bonus: two for one, forgiveness and freedom.

5. Excitement

Excitement is a temporary stirring emotion. It can take you as quickly to the lows as it does highs. There may be exciting moments as a result of your Christ Centered Prayer practice. Yes, it is exciting to taste the fruits of a realized aware consciousness. The more you are living out of your Spiritual Heart Center, the more the natural wondrous adventures may manifest in your daily life.

Moments of excitement are natural, but when the moments are prolonged, the necessary judgment, reason, or common sense decisions are temporarily stifled. The Christ

Centered Prayer practice teaches you to allow even the most exciting moments to pass quickly. Highs and lows are not sustainable. What goes up, must come down!

Excitement may also contain an element of joy. Joy is the one emotion in which the mind revels; consequently, many opportunities for mischief abound. The Christ Centered Prayer may transform the excitement emotion with joy to one of sobering contentment. It is better to be content.

6. Fear

Fear is a paralyzing, restrictive emotional force that can limit your ability to act from a balanced state of consciousness. It can be so debilitating that it can override common sense, causing a stumbling block that would prevent you from moving on with your life.

Fear takes you on an emotional roller coaster ride through the house of horrors, walled by distorted mirrors. Fear can hold you prisoner to anxiety that can rise when the truth is attempting to break through years of conditioning.

Fear can hinder your creativity and paralyze your ability to move forward on your spiritual journey. Fear of death, illness, loneliness, or being emotionally or physically hurt may hold you in a warp space of depression. The many fears are incalculable.

You have the power to attach fear to endless situations. You become fearful the moment you face giving up that for which you have spent most of your lifetime protecting: friends, position, or wealth.

Fear attaches to that which does not permanently exist. You are constantly being asked to give up the emotional *attachment* to the transient things of this world, not the *use* of them. Giving up the attachment can be more difficult than giving up any*thing* or any*one*.

The Christ Centered Prayer practice allows you to realize that all is replaceable and that everything of this world is for your use. Position, cars, and homes are all for your use. No *thing* is permanent. All is relative to this plane; therefore, all rises and all falls in relative time and space.

Hold fast to your practice commitment. When a choice rises, you have the option of making it in fear or freedom. The antidote for fear is love. Sow seeds of love. "There is no fear in love; but perfect love casteth out fear: because fear hath torment. He that feareth is not made perfect in love" (1 John 4:18).

7. Fright

Fright is an anxious moment when you dread to move forward toward an individual or situation. As you progress with your Christ Centered Prayer practice, you may find that you have the courage to meet others and do the things you never expected.

A little fright may serve a valuable purpose. A little stage fright does not prevent you from moving forward. It may even help you do what is necessary. The more you practice the Christ Centered Prayer, the more fright may subside. You might always have a tinge of fright as you progress. It may help keep the ego from overstepping *its* bounds.

8. Frustration

Frustration rises as an irritating emotional energy. It usually rises when you experience a drought in your life or when you are prevented from doing something you want to do. The distractions of this world can cause it to be difficult for you to maintain a peaceful calm in your life. Thus, frustrations begin.

Your perseverance and sincerity with your Christ Centered Prayer practice may overcome any frustration. Do not dialogue with the frustrating emotional disturbances during or after your prayer practice. If frustration is causing tears to flow, allow them; crying is purifying.

Be gentle and especially loving with yourself. A yearning, aching heart for the Christ will move you inward. During these times, be more patient and persistent with your prayer practice. Return to the inner calm.

9. Grief

Grief is a gut-wrenching emotion. It will rise to penetrate your heart and torment your life. It may rise to fill a temporary vacuum that loss created. It is your attachment to grief that causes suffering and keeps you from moving beyond it. Grief is yours to do with as you wish.

Grief is no respecter of individual expressions of consciousness. It stalks all. Grief can hold you intently focused on your perceived loss. This may produce sporadic involuntary tearing and crying. Accept, allow, and respect grief's relative comings and goings.

No one, no matter how sympathetic he or she is, can enter

your space of rising, sorrowful, emotional intensity. Grief may not easily pass. It may cling for a time then subside and fade in the background only to rise again at intervals. Stained with your heartfelt memories, grief may rise again and again to trigger a reminder of your loss.

The Christ Centered Prayer practice allows you to experience your grief in a positive love for yourself. You are taught to be aware of its rising and its falling, its coming and going. You accept it for what it is—a rising emotion—then let it go by returning to the awareness of your Spiritual Heart Center area.

You may exorcize your grief outside of your prayer practice by noting exactly what emotion is rising, the intensity, and the sorrow that overshadows your heart. Only dialoguing with and attachment to the rising grief can hold you prisoner to it.

Joy and grief exist in this world of opposites. Because within any opposite is its opposing force, there may be the transformation of the memories from a sorrowful grief to a loving joy. It may occur when you are willing to express sincere gratitude for the time spent, love received, and life shared with the one you have lost.

In gratitude, a loss may become a gain. You are the recipient of all the love expressed, an heir to all that has gone before. You may release your loved one not to a grave, but rather to the awareness of your Spiritual Heart Center. A loving relationship is a gift that remains with the giver and receiver. It is an expression of your being.

Rejoice that you were chosen to share the love and companionship. Celebrate the passing as you did the coming.

You can convert your tears of sorrow to tears of joy by knowing that which touched your heart *is* your heart.

10. Guilt

Guilt rises when you believe you have done something wrong or something hurtful. It is one of the most destructive self-inflicted emotions. Guilt does its greatest damage when it lingers long after time has lapsed or you have made the necessary restitution.

Guilt twists the mind and grieves the heart. The practice of the Christ Centered Prayer may release and purify an obsession with guilt. You have the opportunity to do just that. Guilt is a tormentor that rubs salt in an open wound. Guilt never cured an illness nor solved a problem. Give it up, and get on with your life.

11. Hate

Hate is a self-destructive emotion. It is a negative emotion toward self or others. Anger and fear usually accompany it. Remember that the same emotional expression of hate, once purified, may be expressed as love. Within every emotion lies its opposite. You may use the same energy to hate as you would to love. Imagine this same power of love used as hate. There is no stronger negative emotion than hate expressed in anger with fear. It can devastate the mind and body—yours.

Any negative expression may be purified to its original state during the Christ Centered Prayer practice. This is the power of the Christ Centered Prayer. You choose.

12. Hope

"Hope is a powerful force that freshens the internal well-spring of your life. It softens each step of your inner walk. Hope picks you up after a fall and holds your hand as you continue your inner walk."[1] When your faith has temporarily withered, hope is what allows you to continue your spiritual walk on the straight and narrow path.

Hope carries you through the mysterious shadows of doubts and dark nights of the soul. It gives you permission to get over, around, or through the obstacles on your path. Hope keeps you strong enough to take the next step *and* the next step; the Christ Centered Prayer is with you every step of the way.

13. Humor

Humor is an emotion that allows you to appreciate the comical in stressful situations. It may lighten a serious situation. Humor is one of the best relaxers, and it may improve your health.

Maintaining a sense of humor is important. In times of sadness, learn to laugh at the obvious foolishness of this world. It may keep you from getting caught up in its illusions. This life's journey is difficult enough, but without an appreciation for the comical, it is next to impossible.

---

1 Carla R. Mancari, *The Minute Method: It's Life Changing! Realize Your Full Potential* (Tucson: Wheatmark, 2012), 99.

14. Inner Joy

Inner joy is an uplifting feeling. It is the gift that is never giddy or pretentious. An abiding joy exists in being consciously aware of your Spiritual Heart Center. Unlike the outer joy in a world of achieving worldly pursuits, the inner contentment comes with an inner joy as you are established in the presence of the Christ.

Once you have experienced this inner joy, it adds color to your outer world. To lose the inner joy would be to return to a black-and-white world. Inner joy rests in a peace beyond understanding. It is a soft feeling that sees you through the sadness of worldly events.

15. Love

You will find as many definitions of love as there are individuals who express it one moment and withdraw it the next. Precisely because love can turn on a dime, it is difficult to define.

Poets write about one sort of love. Romance novels are full of it. You can use and misuse love and yet seldom understand it. You may withhold it as though it were a coin in your pocket to spend whenever you please, or not. Coins are useless unless you spend them. Love is worthless unless you express it.

Love may bask in the rays of the sun or hide in the shadow of the night. Love is a force to be reckoned with when used for good or ill. This question may rise: Is there an *if*? "I will love you, *if* you love me." That is called commercial love.

Commercial love laden with all of the *ifs* is mired in a slush of attachments and costs.

The list of *ifs* is endless. I will love you *if* you stay, *if* you do as I say, *if* you will change, *if* you put up with my abuse, *if* you never disagree with me, etc. You may have many more *ifs* to add to the list. This world is replete with love's *ifs*, and they may come in multiple disguises.

The Christ Centered Prayer may deepen your hearing ability and help you recognize the *ifs* and realize that beyond all of the *ifs* is divine love. An unconditional love knows no *ifs*. It knows its beloved, you, and embraces you under all circumstances.

16. Pleasure

Pleasure is a delightful, pleasing feeling. It is the experience that may occur as inner insights, revelations, or realizations rise during a Christ Centered Prayer practice. The pleasure experience may translate to contentment in your daily life activities. However, if you have an attachment to pleasure for its sake, in its absence, it may express its opposite, pain.

17. Regret

Regret rises with a mistaken thought, word, or deed against yourself or others. Regret has a mesmerizing effect on your mind's memory. It holds you in a past that no longer exists. It pains your heart, twists your mind, and holds you in a time warp.

Regret requires your full attention. It will torment you

into believing you should have, or could have, done something differently. When you accept the responsibility for having done harm to yourself or others, you turn away from the misconduct. You may even make amends. However, constantly revisiting a regret is like constantly replaying a broken record. It causes the needle (you) to get caught in a groove.

Wallowing in regretful sorrow is not productive or necessary. You treat it the same way you treat guilt: notice it, do not deny it, do not dialogue with it, and let it go. The Christ Centered Prayer practice washes regrets in forgiveness and purification. Accept forgiveness. This gives you the freedom to bathe in love's purity.

18. Rejection

There may be a time when rejection by others is overwhelming, and your heart will ache for relief. Your greatest protection from abuse, rudeness, or insults is to practice the Power Prayer (chapter 15) and the Christ Centered Prayer. You come to understand that the abuse by others is their problem, not yours. Those who would reject you and heap rudeness upon you do harm to themselves.

Hold your head high, lead with your heart, and be aware that your best efforts, at times, will not be enough. You are not held accountable for the rejection by others. With the help of the Christ Centered Prayer practice, you may develop the ability to handle rejection. You are then free to live the life you choose.

19. Shame

Shame may rise when you are harboring guilt or regret from conduct others believe unacceptable. Being shamed by authority figures or cultural conditioning may well drag you into the shadows of despair, unworthiness, and loneliness, causing a withdrawal from a world perceived as threatening. Behavioral errors judged by others are not your be-all, end-all.

What others think of you is their issue. Do not give anyone your power to think less of you. Move on, and accept that yours is a forgiving, understanding God. Walk out of the shadows into the light of a warm embrace of the belovedness of your God.

Contents that rise in the mind's states of consciousness are normal, natural responses to life's conditions. Exaggerated, prolonged emotional expressions attached to the mind's contents are not necessary and may deplete energy that could be put to better use. The Christ Centered Prayer practice empowers you to release or save, in your memory bank, an emotional response.

All of the mind's contents must rise, and emotions do have value determined by their circumstances. Repressing an emotion may be as detrimental to you as over-expressing it. The Christ Centered Prayer practice neutralizes and balances the rising contents by teaching you neither to repress nor to deny them. You simply allow them to rise and fall. In time, with practice, you are no longer under the domination of any of the mind's contents.

The Christ Centered Prayer practice of not dialoguing when any content rises, whether positive or negative, gives you the opportunity to be in control. The intensity of any content expressed is the result of complex conditioning; however, that intensity is subject to your modification.

A contented life requires that all phases of your life be emotionally balanced. The Christ Centered Prayer's no-dialogue, no-response practice allows you to recognize the contents as they rise and establish the necessary balance.

Notice how a content may affect you and how the Christ Centered Prayer practice may make a difference in your daily life. It is to your advantage to recognize a content as it rises. You need never be held captive by any content. It is your choice!

Eight

Expansive Awareness and the Void

Indescribable

There is I, and there is you …
then we are undone.
There is none.
– cm

EXPANSIVE AWARENESS AND the Void are often referred to as realizations. They are not. This is because there is no consciousness to realize either of them, and they have no adequate description. All that we can do is to tell you *about* them.

Expansive Awareness

Beyond all states of consciousness, there is Expansive Awareness of be-ing. There is no transition from the highest state of the Christ consciousness to Expansive Awareness. The consciousness state fades, and being Expansive Awareness remains.

There is emptiness, and yet there is fullness. There is nothing, and yet, everything. You are a spiritual being sojourning in a physical sense form upon this earth, but the greater reality is in the infinite life of God Expansive Awareness.

Expansive Awareness is the light in enlightenment. It is the light come into the world, and the darkness could not overcome it. It is the journey home spoken of from all ages. "And the light shineth in darkness; and the darkness comprehended it not" (John 1:5).

There is no beginning and no ending when being Expansive Awareness. For a golden moment the reality of being is expressed in silent Expansive Awareness. The descending path recurs when the Christ consciousness rises.

Within Expansive Awareness, the preexistent "Word" spontaneously rises, and through it all things are made. "All things were made by him; and without him was not any thing made that was made" (John 1:3).

Once awakened to the truth of *no person,* there is no person to suffer or to die. The *I* is a tool of communication, not identification. Recognition of your truth is real freedom. "And ye shall know the truth, and the truth shall make you free" (John 8:32).

Reverend Sandy attempts to explain her existence as Expansive Awareness. She had to live with the Expansive Awareness of be-ing for more than a year before she attempted to put it into words:

> Working and moving backward from the understandable yet mistaken attachment to a separate individual false sense of self (called "Sandy") and its corresponding feelings of alienation and suffering to, being one aware, is true freedom and eternal life. That truth, for me, is awareness of oneness, be-ing.
>
> The subsequent realization of consciousness rising in awareness clarifies the long quoted "unity in diversity," "trinity," or "three in one" so commonly referred to in our tradition as mystery. I agree mystery is mysterious, but it is not unreal. Granted, it cannot be "grasped" by the mind because it transcends the mind. As we know, mind, senses, reason, will, intellect, and memory all rise within conscious awareness, but they are not "awareness."
>
> This truth has been further clarified as Christ

consciousness rising within awareness. In Christ consciousness there is no darkness, no separation, no alienation, no suffering, and no death. There is simply the Christ, the Word of God, the Holy One of God in whom there is no other. This one, truth, life, and light came quite unexpectedly during a silent prayer period with my teacher.

I experienced myself moving from my usual separate personal sense of being "Sandy" into a realization of oneness in Christ consciousness and then dissolving within through this oneness to the be-ing Expansive Awareness.

In a very real way, all must awaken from the identification with an individual, personal separate sense of being to the oneness of the awareness of the Christ consciousness where Jesus Christ is one in His Father. This is to know the Father as Jesus knows the Father. Jesus is the way, and the way to the Father is through Him.

This is no longer a platitude for me but a direct truth. Sandy to Jesus and through Jesus to the Father consciousness, to Expansive Awareness: being without being aware "of" anything or anyone. It is the journey home spoken of from all ages.

This truth unfolded during a silent prayer session with my teacher. I was aware of becoming smaller and smaller as an individual personal sense of Sandy until "I" ultimately disappeared, dissolving completely. Gone. What remained had

> no object of perception, no personal separate sense, just be-ing Expansive Awareness, being without being conscious "of" anything or anyone....
>
> It has also taken more than a year to begin to assimilate and articulate in words how Expansive Awareness has led to an understanding and wisdom, wisdom I continue to grow into. Awareness is the light in "enlightenment." It is the light, I might add, that has never been extinguished, nor can it be. It is the "light" of awareness that shines in the darkness, and the darkness cannot overcome it. It is the light in Jesus's "I am" statement so often quoted in the Gospel of John. It is the light come into the world.[1]

Expansive Awareness is difficult to put into words because words are not it. Taking the time and living with the reality of being it, as Reverend Sandy did, was the wise thing to do.

Mary attempts to put into words the indescribable. The Expansive Awareness effect is profound:

> I moved to the Christ Consciousness. One with myself, one with oneness, so comfortable, so whole. The Christ consciousness fades to being Expansive Awareness.
>
> Upon returning to my individual state of con-

1 Ibid., unpublished.

> sciousness, I was aware of healing, purification, and forgiveness. I realized the power of the Spiritual Heart Center and that the purifying of energy provides more capacity to love unconditionally. A power beyond anything the mind can conjure or conceive.
>
> I had a profound sense of unconditional love flowing through me. I was in love with everything and aware of love in all things. I had an awareness that judging puts an iron gate before a loving heart.

Mary's be-ing Expansive Awareness leaves her with a greater understanding of unconditional love. She is impressed with the negative effects of judging.

Expansive Awareness is beyond Christ consciousness. There is no *I*, no *person*. The *I*, or *person*, has no reality, so why create one? "Thou shalt not make unto thee any graven image, or any likeness of any thing that is in heaven above, or that is in the earth beneath, or that is in the water under the earth" (Ex. 20:4).

The Void

The Void is not void-less. It is the Almighty indescribable God from which all proceeds. You can only be totally amazed at the wonder of it. "He stretcheth out the north over the empty place, and hangeth the earth upon nothing" (Job 26:7).

You may be surprised and confused that there is this Void God. Your first inclination is to describe it to yourself: not possible. You struggle to understand it; you cannot. You struggle to talk about it; you cannot.

As you return from the Void, you know that you know the unknown, the almighty Void God none can describe. Once known, you know it will be for others to venture within, to know they know for themselves.

You are left with the knowing there are two types of individuals: the one who knows the Void God and *cannot* describe it and the one who does not know the Void God and can describe it.

The almighty Void God is truly all in all and beyond all description. The Supreme Being is beyond words, thoughts, consciousness, and awareness. Whatever you can imagine it *is*, it is *not*. Whatever you say it *is*, it is *not*.

Reverend Sandy was constantly wanting a definition of the Void. She would try in many ways to trick my giving her one; it never worked. When she found out for herself, the tricks were over:

> Oh, oh, oh, how long I waited for the Void and the no-thing-ness. This is a strange, strange journey full of twists and turns. How many times I wondered what "pure transcendence" would be like and now I am told by my teacher not to get carried away with it to the point of desiring to go off into the void.

I was not trying to let go and go there, I just went there. I was on a nine-day private intensive retreat with a rigorous schedule of silent prayer and solitude. I was simply practicing the silent Christ Centered Prayer as my teacher had instructed. As thoughts, emotions, and sensations rose, I simply again became aware of my Spiritual Heart Center area. Nothing more, nothing less. I returned and rested in awareness.

After three days of intense silence, I was just sitting there, and without warning, without fanfare, without doing anything, it just happened. I just slipped from awareness into the void. I was looking at the light of consciousness on the inner screen, and the next thing I knew I was coming up from a deep place not knowing how I got there, how long I'd been there, or even remembering wanting to go there. Yes, the Void is indescribable.

The Void surely made an impact on my life. Coming off the retreat I noticed people were strangely beautiful. I found myself perceiving goodness in people in whom I previously saw nothing to commend. Now they seemed full of potential.

Perhaps it was simply that my potential was expanding. I was amazed at myself. The sharp edge was not there, I was relating more kindly and the world seemed to be relating to me more kindly.

Returning to the hectic demands of a house-

> holder and priest, I carried with me a sense of awe and gratitude. Nothing had changed, but everything had changed. It would take years for the event to be integrated and to settle. It has taken years for me to put pen to paper about this retreat. I speak of it now simply to say the Void exists.
>
> I am now aware, in retrospect, that its value is not in "itself" an end, but rather, one means in more fully understanding and appreciating in this life some of the mystery of God. This mystery to be lived fully in each individual life as compassion, mercy, peace, justice, and unconditional love.[2]

Reverend Sandy now understood why the Void was indescribable. She, too, could not put it into words. She finally settled for "knowing she knew."

Saying how either the Expansive Awareness or the Void may affect an individual can be difficult. Some are in a daze, and some are left dumbfounded for a time. Others have reported frustration and the inability to describe them. No matter the effects, Expansive Awareness or the Void is what it is, and it remains the Expansive Awareness and the Almighty God Void that many truth seekers venture forth to know.

This entire chapter is about Expansive Awareness and

---

2 Sandra Casey-Martus and Carla Mancari, *The Lessons: How to Understand Spiritual Principles, Spiritual Activities, and Rising Emotions, Volume One* (Tucson: Wheatmark, 2008), 203–204.

the Void God, but not one word describes them. Expansive Awareness and the Void simply are. "And this is life eternal, that they might know thee the only true God, and Jesus Christ, whom thou hast sent" (John 17:3).

Nine

Insights, Revelations, and Realizations

The Differences

Beyond a mind at rest,
the Holy Spirit will reveal . . .
all things real.
– cm

THE CHRIST CENTERED Prayer method includes insights, revelations, and realizations. Subtle but important differences reside among them. "As for me, I will behold thy face in righteousness: I shall be satisfied, when I awake, with thy likeness" (Ps. 17:15).

Insights

An insight you get and may fade over time. Insights rise in the mind state of consciousness. They are moments of intellectual understanding. Insights may make a positive contribution as you progress on your spiritual journey. Insights may rise in the mind while processing memories or during times of contemplative rest. Like experiences, insights may fade only later to be recalled—or not.

Insights may sustain your spiritual journey when something tempts you to wander off the spiritual path. They may move you in the direction where revelations and realizations rise. An insight is a match that may light a fire. Insights have great value.

Revelations

A revelation is a gift that confirms truth's existence. Revelations open the door to realizations that resolve divine mysteries (the Holy Trinity). Revelation may reveal the Holy Trinity's oneness and the participation of each individual member of the Holy Trinity.

Revelations reveal truth through a greater inner vision. Revelations are about the truth. They may define, explain, and clarify the mystery we call God.

A revelation if neglected, may recede, but it does not go away. It will return to tug at your heartstrings another time.

Private revelation never contradicts a previously accepted historic revelation. It edifies and builds up the community of the faithful. Revelations may lead to realizations that awaken you to all that you are.

Realizations

Realization, or enlightenment, is a common word used on the spiritual journey. In reality there is never any *you* to realize anything. As progression on a spiritual journey occurs, an awakening, referred to as a realization, may occur.

Realizations are your nature. They confirm that eternal life is not a destination or a place. Eternal life cannot be housed or destroyed. Here and now is as good a time as any to realize eternal life. "And this is life eternal, that they might know thee the only true God, and Jesus Christ, whom thou hast sent" (John 17:3).

It is not necessary to remember or recall a realized truth because *you are it.* Being a realized truth, in the present, does not require a memory. There is no need to remember that which you are in the present. A realization is not a past experience or a past insight. A realization is the present. Memory requires a past.

A realization of the truth enables you to recognize temptations for what they are and overcome them. You are aware that your strength is of the Lord God. You find you are no longer easily caught up in the chatter of this world. "Let my mouth be filled with thy praise and with thy honor all the day" (Ps. 71:8).

Not always timed according to plan, a realization may rise when least expected. Do not be quick to think that there is only one realization. There is not one grand realization. In reality many realizations constitute being a fully realized (awakened) being.

Realizations transform faith into belief. With each realization, truth penetrates the ignorance perpetuated by the illusionary world of your imagination. Realizations cast a light of understanding within the reality of your being. "The wisdom of the prudent is to understand his way: but the folly of fools is deceit" (Prov. 14:8).

Reverend Sandy shares her progress from a limited black-and-white world to a world in color. The realizations make the difference:

> Consciousness is certainly an interesting phenomenon. At the start of my spiritual journey, like many folks, I thought of human existence in terms of being conscious or unconscious, alive or dead!
>
> I certainly had a notion of the waking state, dreaming state, and deep sleep states of consciousness, but that was about it. Concepts like transcendence, eternal life, resurrection, after life, and life after life held a certain curiosity, appeal, and fascination but hardly registered with any certainty of experience on my inner screen.

I am now happy to report, like Shakespeare, there really is, "more than meets the eye." Or Paul, "But as it is written, Eye hath not seen, nor ear heard, neither have entered into the heart of man, the things which God hath prepared for them that love him" (1 Cor. 2:9).

In looking back, I remember one trip over the Teton Pass in Wyoming on a beautiful sunny winter day. The trees were shining and the light was beautiful. As I approached the 10 percent grade, I had the very clear realization experience of a silent inner witness to the beauty in the midst of attending to the winding road, double white passing lines, and guard rails. The thought rose: *Is that it? Is that enlightenment? Is that the "whisper passing by the cave"? That?* I remember laughing out loud. I had expected something a lot more spectacular for sure.

The silent abiding sense of being awake inside in the midst of all other activities certainly came with no bells or cymbals announcing, "You have arrived!" This was all quite effortless, normal, quiet, and natural. Isn't that what all the famous masters say—"Oh, it is really nothing, and you don't have to do anything…" Of course, that is after they have spent decades fasting, meditating, studying, serving, and waiting patiently, preparing for such a natural unfolding!

Over the years I have come to realize that what we typically call "Enlightenment" is really

> a cumulative series of little realizations of truth of your being over a long period of time.[1]

Although Reverend Sandy was caught by surprise from the simplicity of a realization, she was able to maintain a sense of humor. A sense of humor can go a long way on a spiritual journey.

Insights, revelations, and realization rise when you are ready and prepared to receive them. To rush or force, prematurely, any spiritual activity may cause physical, psychological, or spiritual harm. Preparation for your inner journey comes in many forms. The Christ Centered Prayer practice prepares and readies you to receive insights, revelations, and realizations that disallow any attempt to capture, codify, or commercialize eternal life.

An established unshaken certainty of your God nature is the fruit of a faithful practice of the Christ Centered Prayer. The Christ Centered Prayer practice is the straight gate and narrow way that is paved with insights, revelations, and realizations.

Practice the Christ Centered Prayer, become aware of your Spiritual Heart Center, and you may find your existence before birth and after death—the eternity you never left. "Keep thy heart with all diligence; for out of it are the issues of life" (Prov. 4:23).

1 Ibid., 74–75.

Ten

Realizations, Part One

Your Nature

Greater is the view.
Darkness to light.
All things new.
– cm

THE PREVIOUS CHAPTER discussed the differences among insights, revelations, and realizations. Reviewed in this chapter, part one, and the next chapter, part two, are realizations. There are a number of realizations, some subtle, some not so subtle. Nevertheless, in the Christ Centered Prayer method, they are all-inclusive.

Realizations awaken you to the full awareness of the reality of being. This world of opposites exists within consciousness that is real only in a relative sense. "And that, knowing the time, that now it is high time to awake out of sleep: for now is our salvation nearer than when we believed" (Rom. 13:11).

Realizations are uniquely tailored for each individual. The Christ Centered Prayer practice may gradually fine-tune you to receive the necessary realizations. You never have a reason to compare or envy another's spiritual path. Be convinced yours is perfect for you.

The following are brief descriptions of the different realizations that may occur as a result of the Christ Centered Prayer practice. Any may occur. They occur when a particular readiness and a need for them exist. Realizations do not follow a prescribed sequence.

The Individual Expression of Mind-Body Consciousness Realization

From the one Christ consciousness rise many individual expressions of (not separate from) mind-body states of consciousness, one of which is yours. Your individual expression of mind-body states of consciousness changes according to your physical growth, thoughts, words, and deeds.

As you practice the Christ Centered Prayer method, you may realize your mind-body states of consciousness. You may become aware as your consciousnesss changes from the mind (thoughts) state to the body (physical) state of consciousness.

The individual expression of the mind-body states of consciousness are the easiest to realize. In fact, you probably may be conscious of your mind and body most of the time. The Christ Centered Prayer practice heightens the awareness of the mind and body states of consciousness.

It is within the mind's state of consciousness that a sense of a physical body rises. The mind consciousness (thoughts, feelings, with the five senses) creates a sense of a separate self-identity. Attachment to and identification with the sense of a separate self leads to a mistaken personal sense of self. To attach and identify with this separate sense of self is the first step in the creation of the illusionary belief that a separate self exists—the self of *I*, *mine*, and *me*!

On this earth plane, the body as an expression of mind's consciousness vibrates at an energy frequency that enables the body to be seen and sensed as a solid form. As you falsely identify with the mind, you falsely identify with a physical body separate from other individual expressions of mind-body consciousness.

The false sense of a separate mind and body is the easiest vibratory energy to get attached to. The false sense of a separate, personal body to defend, in fear of harm or dying, may cause a perceptual gap difficult to venture beyond. In reality there is no time or space. In reality you are an individual expression of the one Christ consciousness.

Reverend Sandy shares her unexpected realization of the unmanifested vibrating energy. She was able to realize that the light without was also the light within her:

> It was the 4th Sunday of Pentecost. I was kneeling for the Confession of Sin after the Creed. We were behind the high altar where the light is dim, and the rector and I were mostly hidden.
>
> I had my eyes closed, as is my custom. Peering inside of my eyelids, my common everyday awareness of the array of light and motion offered no distraction to my prayer. What did grab my attention in a most powerful yet subtle way was a realization that the inner landscape participated in the outer landscape without change or distinction.
>
> I had not previously been aware of that until this strange morning. I thought it must be the lighting. After numerous "tests" of my perception, I became convinced that I actually perceived something about consciousness that I had not been consciously aware of before—energy in motion.
>
> I am not suggesting the energy was "now in manifested flesh appearing" as if it just suddenly appeared on the scene. I was now for the first time able to see it, eyes opened, eyes closed, and realized it as unmanifested vibrating energy.

I tested this over and over by ever so slowly having a sense of the light and its exact substance (sort of like light dancing particles). I carefully opened my eyes to behold eyes open what I had, in fact, been viewing interiorly when my eyelids were shut tight. It seemed I was seeing through my eyes closed, and I knew it.

I realized in an instant that there was no empty space. There existed between the rector and me, kneeling on either side of the altar, a pregnant field of lively vibrating energy that filled the entire altar area. If I had a sharp enough knife, it could be cut.

Then I realized that the only thing at all that was really in that church was a massive energy field of vibrating consciousness at various speeds. Some wood, some metal, some bread, some wine, some song, some bodies, and yet, all one gigantic living breathing pulsating dancing Light.

I knew experientially the meaning behind Jesus's statement, "I am the Light," in a new and most delightful way. I also knew that in some mysterious, and also not so mysterious, way we all dance in that Light and, in fact, we are that Light.[1]

Being a sceptic, Reverend Sandy had to put the real-

1 Sandra Casey-Martus and Carla Mancari, *The Lessons: How to Understand Spiritual Principles, Spiritual Activities, and Rising Emotions, Volume One* (Tucson: Wheatmark, 2008), 79.

ization to a test. However, her consciousness continued to manifests the spaceless field of vibrating energy until she was able to realize the oneness of the light.

Realization of your individual expression of your mind-body states of consciousness may awaken, or stir, an interest in a spiritual journey. At the core of your being is the nagging knowledge that "there is more."

The Christ Consciousness Realization

For the followers of Jesus Christ, there is one "Father" Christ consciousness expressing as individual (not separate) expressions of consciousness. "There is one body, and one Spirit, even as ye are called in one hope of your calling; One Lord, one faith, one baptism, One God and Father of all, who is above all, and through all, and in you all" (Eph. 4:4–6).

As your energy speeds up, you ascend from your body, mind, and individual expression of consciousness to the higher states of the Christ consciousness. There is no *I* or *you* in the highest state of the Christ consciousness; however, the realization is in consciousness.

There is just the conscious awareness of *be-ing* Christ consciousness without a self-identity. The thought of separation is just a thought and has no basis in reality. Realizing the Christ consciousness removes the illusionary sense of separation. Realize the Christ consciousness, and all sense of separation fades. There is only one Christ consciousness.

Once you have shattered self-identification with the separate false sense of mind, body, and individual consciousness, you have traveled beyond the false concepts that have held you captive. "I in them, and thou in me, that they may be made perfect in one; and that the world may know that thou hast sent me, and hast loved them, as thou hast loved me" (John 17:23).

The Spiritual Principle of Supply Realization

There exists a spiritual principle of supply, one that meets your needs—need, not greed. In the awareness of your "God source" is your spiritual supply. All that is necessary to meet your needs already exists.

Your supply is a God source that always exists in unmanifested abundance. It is limitless in its unmanifested source state. It can never be depleted. Money, food, objects, or persons—these are not your spiritual supply source. These are a few of the forms that the spiritual principle of supply may manifest. The peace, joy, comfort, and material supply that you need and seek exist within you.

You may realize the spiritual principle of supply with the Christ Centered Prayer practice. As your practice progresses, a consciousness of the manifestation of your needs become more recognizable.

Look around. This earth produces all you shall ever need. The Lord is *not* the one who limits supply or causes hunger. It is the human manipulation of the spiritual supply manifestation. "Be not ye therefore like unto them: for your Father knoweth what things ye have need of before ye ask him" (Matt. 6:8).[2]

---

2 Sandra Casey-Martus and Carla Mancari, *Your "Other Heart": The Best-Kept Secret* (Tucson: Wheatmark, 2010), 50.

The mind is powerful, but it may also be mischievous and can cause havoc on the plane of opposites. "Mentally focusing your thoughts in order to fulfill your needs is incompatible with a harmonious spiritual nature—yours. 'Because the carnal mind is enmity against God: for it is not subject to the law of God, neither indeed can be' (Rom. 8:7)"[3]

Until you begin the return journey from your immersion in the world of conditioning, you lack the realization that the source of all supply is beyond the mental state. You believe that you are separated and on your own. You are *not* alone. You are an individual expression of your God being, not a separate and apart being.

Your supply may appear as persons, objects, and events. Because this is the plane of opposites, you may attract and be attracted to both the positive and the negative forms that consciousness manifest. Some you will want, and some you will not want.

With the Christ Centered Prayer practice, you may come to realize your "God source" and resting in the awareness of your Spiritual Heart Center area allows the things of this world to be appreciated and accepted for what they are, gifts to be enjoyed. Your response to them can then be heartfelt gratitude rather than insatiable greed."[4] Choose wisely.

The spiritual principle of supply was a difficult lesson for Reverend Sandy to realize. She realized it the hard way:

3 Ibid., 49.
4 Ibid., 53.

I had the opportunity to travel to France. I was gifted with a coach "Buddy Pass" to fly standby. My ticket cost forty-four dollars. I actually gloated to think that I could get by so cheaply. I had the money for a round-trip first-class ticket but chose not to spend it on myself.

I had no difficulty getting to France and was as pleased with myself as I could be. Until... the day came to fly home standby. In the Paris airport, I waited for my name to be called for my flight. What I did not know was that there were about fifteen folks with greater seniority doing exactly the same thing!

I began to get a taste of reality. Getting back to the USA was not going to be a piece of cake. It was the sixteenth of July. I was alone in the airport, and all of the flights for the USA had taken off. I had to find a hotel for the night and begin waiting again at 6:00 a.m. the next morning.

The next morning began another long day in the Paris airport. I was tired, discouraged, and rapidly running out of cash. I asked the attended, "When does it look like I may get on a flight?"

"August," the attendant replied. The only way I could get home now was to buy a one-way coach ticket. It cost $2,550. I was finally going home. Exhausted and sitting in the rear of the plane, after two days of trial, I let out a huge laugh. I remembered the spiritual principle of supply.

I realized in a flash what I had done. I had

> the money. My need had been met abundantly, but I had chosen to disregard and not accept that which had been prepared. Instead, I had spent my mental energy focused on getting to France on the cheap. I attracted exactly what I believed I wanted, but I ended up pinched in the pocket and totally humiliated....
>
> Taking thought to attract my need was not necessary. I finally realized that money was only one of the forms that my source of supply manifest for my use. I realized this the hard way, but I realized it.[5]

This was a hard lesson, but it was one that Reverend Sandy did come to value. She realized that the spiritual principle of supply takes many forms. Money is only one of them.

If what you have matches your present need, but you use less of it in fear that there may not be more, there may not be more. To hold back, not enjoy, or not share reasonably all that manifests is unnecessary.

The Split-Soul Realization

An individual soul-consciousness rises within the Christ Consciousness. It descends to the earth plane of opposites,

---

5 Sandra Casey-Martus and Carla Mancari, *The Lessons: How to Understand Spiritual Principles, Spiritual Activities, and Rising Emotions, Volume One* (Tucson: Wheatmark, 2008), 181–182.

and it splits as male and female. "Have you not read that the one who made them at the beginning made them 'male and female'" (Matthew 19:4).

Each split-half goes its separate way experiencing male and female forms. In one particular time and space, the split-halves awaken to their original oneness in the Christ Consciousness. An individual soul-consciousness spiritually reuniting as opposites, or same sex, is not a hindrance to the wakening process. The transitional occurrence rises above the physical.

There are those who refer to the split-halve as their soul mate. They are not. The split-halves are actually one soul in the reality of their being. There is only the one soul meeting *itself.* This explains why not judging is important. "Judge not, that ye be not judged" (Matthew 7:1).

Eleven

Realizations, Part Two

Your Nature

The shadows are gone.
The light is always on.
– cm

THIS CHAPTER IS the continuation of the realizations that are all-inclusive for those who practice the Christ Centered Prayer method. Realizations do not rise in any specific order. Individual states of consciousness realizations progress according to the individual's readiness, preparedness, and need.

The Detachment Realization

Attachment is that which causes suffering, binds you to this world, and limits freedom of being. The moment you think *I*, *me*, *my*, and *mine*, attachment rises, and it cause suffering. Attachment of any kind is the unnecessary misuse of energy.

The belief that you exist as a separate person allows attachment to come into existence. In reality, there is not any time when you are not one as your God source. You need not cling to anything created. "For in him we live, and move, and have our being; as certain also of your own poets have said, For we too are his offspring" (Acts 17:28).

Thoughts rise constantly. They are vibrating energy rising as thinking—no more, no less. Thoughts in and of themselves have no emotions attached to them. You attach the conditioned descriptive judgment of good, bad, pleasurable, or painful. The attachment to pleasure can be a subtle pull in its direction. Interestingly, there are seldom, if ever, any complaints about the emotions that give pleasure; however, the rising energy is the same for pain.

One thought is no different from another. Vibrating energy is vibrating energy. Thoughts take the form and conditions that you create for them. In reality there are never any differences and never any opposites. Within the opposite is the opposite. The emotional differences attached to the rising of thoughts are based in past conditioned memory experiences.

Detachment may be realized either from bottom up (pure awareness) or top down Christ consciousness. Bottom up requires an observer. Top down does not because none exists. Either type of detachment realization gives freedom from attachment allowing relationships and the use of the things in this world to be enjoyed without suffering.

The Bottom-Up Detachment Realization

The bottom-up detachment practice, is occurring during a Christ Centered Prayer practice every time a thought, image, or emotion rises and you do not dialogue or engage. You are simply an observer.

Detachment from the bottom-up is gradually occurring. It is subtle, and the detachment realization occurs when you, as the observer, drop away. What remains is pure awareness of being. In pure awareness of being, there are no labels, there is no conditioning, and there is no *you*.

Reverend Sandy shares another airport experience. After having missed her plane, she was careful to time her prayer period. As the prayer period ended, Sandy slipped into the detachment realization:

> Due to my focused attention on a Lesson Paper (*The Lessons, Volume One*), I had not heard

my name called for boarding my airplane and consequently missed my plane. However, I was strangely accepting of having missed my plane. I didn't think it would "fly" to try and explain to the stewardess that I was deep in focused attention on a spiritual lesson paper concerning attention when I failed to be attentive to the boarding call, so I sat quietly down to await the next plane an hour away.

I decided since I was tired from all the excitement, I would carefully pray for a while. This time, mindful of security, I sat comfortably on my purse, placed my feet on my luggage, and with my alarm clock by my side, set to signal after a thirty-minute prayer period, it would be just fine. I was backed up this time.

As I began to come out of my prayer period, there was the very clear experience of the sense of hearing rising. The experience of hearing immediately rose. Just hearing sounds, that's all, one sound after another. For a few moments, there was no conditioning associated with the immediacy of the sense of hearing.

Moving out of conscious awareness, the experience of mind rising within consciousness was crystal clear. Then closely behind hearing, rose mind's interpretation of the sounds and language that suddenly was on the horizon. Then after the interpretation of hearing and language registered, the "I" translated the sounds based on my condi-

> tioning and "I" understood what was being said all around "me."
>
> For those few moments before the "I" rose, "I" was not. Detachment moved to attachment. First, the sense of hearing was rising. Then my conscious mind rose with intellect to interpret. Then Sandy wasn't missing her plane! I was really excited because although I had similar experiences of detachment, a little less flashy, this one was crystal clear.
>
> Had "Sandy" not risen with "her sense of herself," I am sure that the fact of hearing, seeing, touching, tasting, smelling, etcetera would simply continue on unencumbered and unhampered by expectations, reason, intellect, discrimination, identity, or cultural conditioning....
>
> I realized exactly what was meant by senses rising and falling, mind rising in consciousness, consciousness rising in awareness, and a separate false sense of self rising.... I also knew how important it is for me not to mistake the conditioned separate sense of self called "Sandy" for the one eternally aware impersonal reality that neither rises nor falls but exists always.... A mistake but also a huge mistake. Who "Sandy" really is, is "Who she is. There is no other."[6]

Fortunately, all turned out well for Reverend Sandy. She was able to get the next flight out and left with an assurance

6 Ibid., 63.

of her reality. However, you are cautioned not to do an inner meditation practice whenever your safety is at risk. Doing a meditation practice in a public place is risky.

The Top-Down Christ Consciousness Detachment Realization

The top-down detachment realization may occur during a realization of the Christ consciousness finest vibratory state. Once the state of Christ consciousness is realized and *it* fades, the Expansive Awareness of be-ing exists (chapter 8). No observer is required for the top-down detachment realization to occur.

While Expansive Awareness is *be-ing*, the Christ consciousness state again rises without an observer. The awareness of the states of individual consciousness, mind consciousness, and body consciousness rise and fall. The realization of the top-down detachment is possible when you are ready and prepared.

Reverend Sandy's plans did not always work out according to her expectations. She had to readjust her thinking and obey when she came for a retreat/vacation visit with me in Florida. The results, for her, were life changing:

> I spent two weeks in Florida with my teacher as part of a retreat/vacation.... The first week I wanted to rest, pray, and reflect. The second week

I wanted to spend some time at the ocean. My teacher had other plans for me.

The second morning I was given an arduous detachment practice instruction. I entered the silence and took the role of an "observer." I increased the frequency and length of my meditation periods, and I ate simply....

I was not accustomed to the intensity of this practice and found it difficult and fatiguing. Having the observer drop away seemed to me to be light years away, and it became increasingly apparent that it would be a result of utter exhaustion.

On the third day of the practice, I was showing signs of distress, and my teacher instructed that I stop the practice. Relieved and appreciative, I felt the weight of the practice had been lifted. Once again I returned to my familiar Christ Centered Prayer practice and rested in awareness. It gave me a much needed sense of relief.

My teacher continued to work with me and on the fourth day while being Expansive Awareness, she instructed me to allow the Christ consciousness to rise and fall. The finest vibration rose and the other states of consciousness were rising and falling. Becoming aware of the Christ consciousness rising and the other states of consciousness rising and falling seemed to be natural, and it was occurring without the benefit of an observer.

It was unexpected, without precedence,

profound, clear, and unmistakable.... Instead of realizing detachment from the "bottom up," the detachment realization came in utter simplicity from the "top down." While this realization was going on, there was no personal sense at all. The clarity of Christ consciousness detachment without effort was realized. The observer did not fade. It never existed in the first place....

Jesus clearly revealed "no word, no observer" were necessary. No "word" for the Christ Centered Prayer practice and no "observer" for the "top-down" Christ consciousness detachment realization.... The discipline of letting go of the rising thoughts, sensations, and emotions (without the use of a word, phrase, image, or breath) in the Christ Centered Prayer, and returning again and again to the awareness of the Spiritual Heart Center area, paves the way for either of the detachment realizations. Like the Christ Centered Prayer, this was a revealed gift of the Holy Spirit in the name of Jesus Christ.

To be detached, for me, did not mean that I was indifferent or aloof, but I found myself strangely aware of the rising thoughts, emotions, sensations, and various streams of consciousness that rose and fell at any given moment in the day without an "I" attached.

I realized that I had the power to, or not to, attach emotions either positive or negative to rising thoughts. I neither felt like I was a saint nor a sinner. I didn't feel victorious or a failure. I just looked and decided whether or not to bite on a juicy rising thought with its commentary and characters.

For me, coming to the Christ consciousness detachment realization was a catastrophic event that turned the worldly standards on end. Adjusting to the Christ consciousness detachment realization was as unsettling as it must have been when those before us realized that the world wasn't flat, the sun didn't revolve around the earth, energy and matter are interchangeable, and that man could walk on the moon.

Living with detachment has been, at times, disorienting, confusing, and tiring. Initially, it was difficult to even think or conjuror up a sense of "I," and there was a feeling of loss.

There was a tendency for "Me" to speak of "myself" in the third person rather than the first person. Certainly, I used "I" when communicating, but there was a detachment and strangeness about hearing my name. It was not obvious to others, but it was obvious to me....

I had to think if I were hungry or not. If I decided I should eat, I then had trouble deciding what to order. After lunch, I went to my familiar haunt to shop and found myself asking myself what in the world was I doing here. I was trying to hold on to the familiar, and yet there was no "hold."

What I was struggling with and continued

to observe was the way in which decisions were being made. Mind and its habits, patterns of operating, and running the show found itself in a subservient position and the new position of servant caught it off guard. Instead of barreling full speed ahead with little regard to others, mind is being asked to adopt a position of ready alertness and to respond to the needs of the moment as they presented themselves....

> When I think back on how I used to immediately attach emotions to thoughts, I realized how fickle the mind was and how easily I got caught up in it. Now I had a choice to suffer or not. The Christ consciousness detachment realization provided me with that choice.

Reverend Sandy's vacation plans were disappointing when they were short-circuited. However, by having to comply with guidance, Reverend Sandy's consciousness soared to higher heights than she could have imagined, allowing her to realize the Christ consciousness detachment from the top down.

Mary, too, was able to move from the Christ consciousness into Expansive Awareness without the witness. The results also left her out of balanced with her immediate surroundings.

The Christ consciousness drops away to every-

> thing-ness, nothingness, and all-ness to being Expansive Awareness.
>
> Then the Christ consciousness rises and mind and body consciousness rises. Just rising and falling. No labels, no identity.
>
> I returned so detached that, for a time, I could not mentally function very well. I could not read the retreat schedule or comprehend the writing on the schedule. I could not remember if it was Thursday or Friday. I was changed. My consciousness had changed.

Mary was fortunate that her top-down Christ consciousness realization detachment occurred while she was attending a Christ Centered Prayer retreat. She was in a safe, quiet environment that allowed her to adjust to a top down detachment realization.

The starting point for either the bottom-up or the top-down detachment realization is awareness of the Spiritual Heart Center area. The Christ Centered Prayer practice is a gentle practice that may allow either of the detachment realizations to occur effortlessly. However, either way, the detachment when realized may be startling, like an inner earthquake, as Reverend Sandy discovered.

At first, detachment may be experienced as a sense of loss. It is the ultimate loss: dying to the false self, the illusionary sense of a separate personal life. It may be disorienting and take time for a personal sense of self to rise again.

Thinking *I*, *me*, *my*, and *mine* may not be immediately possible. It may feel strange not having any sense of self to cling to for a while. There is just the rising and falling energy. Be patient; this usually will not last long. When it does happen, it is best to stay quiet and muse with it for a while. No immediate physical activity should be assumed. Time to readjust to your surrounding environment may be necessary.

Realizing there is no person can be both devastating and radiantly uplifting. The value of a free, non-suffering, non-attached life gradually unfolds. "He that findeth his life shall lose it: and he that loseth his life for my sake shall find it" (Matt. 10:39).

Detachment does not mean indifference to persons, places, or things. You continue to nurture relationships and use the things of this world. However, a house is a house, a car is a car, a friend is a friend, and a spouse is a spouse without possessiveness or ownership. There is no *my* or *mine*. The material world is simply a playground and marvelous display intended for joy, love, service, and relationship. Never mistake it for the reality of the one God who is its source.

It is not the use of things or relationships of this world that is relinquished but the *attachment to them*. It is not necessary to cling to anything. It is a false belief in possessive ownership that creates the illusion of a separation from God.

Detachment is the freedom from the bondage of heavy burdens. It is to take the easy yoke and find rest. For the things of this world are weighty, and you may have grown weary in the pursuit of them. "Come unto me, all ye that labor and are heavy laden, and I will give you rest" (Matt. 11:28).

Understanding that God is one and there is no other

means the total unraveling and elimination of the attachment to and identification with the created order. When creation is conceived of as permanent, when bodies are perceived of as all there is, power, position, and privilege are thought of as all important.

Yes, living out from your God source requires a reorientation in thought patterns. It requires patience and understanding—*and* a sense of humor. Living in a calm state of being is not numbness. It is living as an aware conscious being, free from the domination of emotional conditioning. Relinquishing all attachments to emotions, not the emotions themselves, allows you the freedom to express unconditional love.

The Truth Realization

All vibrating energy creates sound. All sound originates in silence and stillness. All forms have an individual sound. You possess your own specific, unique, individual vibration. You live and breathe as the image and truth in the oneness of your God source. Truth is what you are.

Practice the Christ Centered Prayer and realize the truth of your reality. "BEHOLD, what manner of love the Father hath bestowed upon us, that we should be called the sons of God: therefore the world knoweth us not, because it knew him not" (1 John 3:1).

An attempt to realize truth outside of yourself is not possible. You must go within to realize the intimate oneness of the Creator of your being. Never mistake the referent for the reality. True, God's nature is expressed in all creation. "All things were made by him; and without him was not any thing made that was made" (John 1:3).

Recognizing that God made all things is the acknowledgment that there is an almighty creating power. Not knowing your God's oneness may be a comfort if you wish to keep God at a distance. "And they said unto Mosses, Speak thou with us, and we will hear: but let not God speak with us, lest we die" (Ex. 20:19).

Truth can neither be defiled, dissected, destroyed, nor indefinitely denied. It can be disguised, overshadowed by sin (ignorance), and judgment. Truth is the reality that endures. To believe that truth lie outside in books and myriad teachings is a form of idol worship. Even the thought of God is not God.

Words do not adequately describe truth; therefore, the mind struggles to understand a reality beyond this world. In time, with the Christ Centered Prayer practice, the mind quiets and accepts that with which it cannot argue. You begin to wake up to your true source. "For the truth's sake, which dwelleth in us, and shall be with us for ever" (2 John 1:2).

You are the truth *in* and *out* of your Christ Centered Prayer practice, awake or asleep. As truth, you are a child of God. Your life is a prayer in action. "The Spirit itself beareth witness with our spirit, that we are the children of God" (Rom. 8:16).

Truth teachings are about truth. They are not truth itself. *You* are truth. The "I am" expresses as the many. You are one of the many. To realize this truth at some point, you must choose one path, one teaching that guides you within.

The Christ Centered Prayer, through the "strait gate and narrow way," allows access to the insights, revelations, and realizations. These may reveal the true nature of your being. All work together to fully awaken you to the truth realization. Throughout scripture God claims you. It is for you to discover the truth of being that responds joyfully to the silent voice of its beloved.

Practice the Christ Centered Prayer, and you may realize your truth through the power and grace of your spiritual God being that fulfills a longing heart. The way home lies within your being. The candies of this world are bittersweet. They are not lasting, nor can they ever fill you as the Christ can. The inner door opens wide. Step inside.

You may find yourself in a conflicted emotional state when any of the realizations occur. A realization may challenge old loyalties and clash between the old and new. They have a way of changing your interest. "But now we are delivered from the law, that being dead wherein we were held; that we should serve in newness of spirit, and not in the oldness of the letter" (Rom. 7:6).

Your present and future plans may appear distant, and the familiar less recognizable. The change may cause a direct conflict with your present relationships, job position, or activities. "Think not that I am come to send peace on earth: I came not to send peace, but a sword" (Matt. 10:34).

The conflict of interest is at its greatest intensity when you harbor an insistence to hold on to the familiar while the new overshadows it. "And he that sat upon the throne said, Behold, I make all things new. And he said unto me, Write: for these words are true and faithful" (Rev. 21:5).

The conflict of interest dissolves when you are able to let go of the familiar, making space for the present new interest that has been born of a greater awareness. "But we all, with open face beholding as in a glass the glory of the Lord, are changed into the same image from glory to glory, even as by the Spirit of the Lord" (2 Cor. 3:18).

Jesus was aware of His God reality. Jesus guides you through the awareness of the many realizations. The Christ Centered Prayer practice assists *you* in following Jesus.

You are so precious that Jesus was willing to lay down His life so that you may pick yours up. Embrace the spiritual nature with which you were created. Jesus's teachings, parables, and promises are recorded in the scriptures so that they may lead you to the realization of your divine origin.

If you have never tasted chocolate ice cream, can you realize what it tastes like from someone talking about its qualities? If you want the taste of it for yourself, what must you do? The same is true of realizations. Telling you about them is not the same as realizing them for yourself.

Twelve

Lazarus Rising
A Rising Dormant Energy

A mighty force,
from bottom up,
runs its course.
– cm

THE LAZARUS RISING is not a realization. It is an awakening of the mighty dormant energy resting at the base of the spine. It is referred to in the East as the kundalini. In Christian scripture, we know it as the Lazarus rising.

The Lazarus rising occurs when the dormant energy ascends from the base of the spine. It ascends through the six spiritual centers culminating at the seventh (crown of the head). In the East, the seven spiritual centers are known as chakras.

The Lazarus rising as recorded in scripture is a profound teaching. "And when he thus had spoken, he cried with a loud voice, Lazarus, come forth. And he that was dead cane forth, bound hand and foot with graveclothes: and his face was bound about with a napkin. Jesus saith unto them, Loose him, and let him go" (John 11:43–44).

Jesus's calling Lazarus to come forth from the dead, at the metaphysical-mystical level, translates as dormant energy ascending from the base of the spine. "Loose him, and let him go," is the untying of the knots (purification as the energy moves through the spiritual centers).

Reverend Sandy shares her Lazarus rising awakening while she was on a ten-day silent prayer retreat. Although she had a little book knowledge about it, what occurred took her by surprise:

> When this experience occurred, it was undeniable. I became aware of the intense energy when it spontaneously began to rise with speed, inten-

tion, and intensity that could not be modified. I simply rode the wave of pulsating energy for several minutes. While the energy circulated in a motion that rose up my spine to the top of my head, circling back up through my feet to my head and around and around. I could see the trail of light completing the circuit.

The energy beams of light were very clearly visible to my opened eyes, and the energy extended out of each of my fingers. It was like a laser of white light, and it was so powerful that I had little control.

The energy came from deep within my own core of which, up until that moment, I had no firsthand experience, although I had read about such an energy in spiritual books. Without my intending, expecting, or manipulating, the energy simply came, appeared, and ran its course.

The muscles in my body had a difficult time containing the intensity of the energy while it was moving. There was a contraction and jerking of my muscles as they accommodated this phenomenon. It was not painful; it was remarkable, and I just sat there in awe of what was taking place, fully aware that in some mysterious way I was being shown something about myself that I had never known before. This was not a dream, not imaginary, not esoteric. This was just Sandy having a peek into a reality she had up to that point never been aware.

When it subsided, I found myself relaxing and had the sense of being energy without boundaries. Of course, I certainly was in my body, and the boundaries were there at the same time as this unbounded spacious sense of an energy field in which I existed also.

The knowledge through this awakening and the assimilation and the integration of it has taken years. On the one hand, it seemed extraordinary, and on the other, it was just a matter of fact. I absolutely knew that I was certainly more than meets the eye.

Awakening to my essential nature, body, mind, and personality was shot through with light and energy certainly re-orientated my understanding of the depth and breadth of the fact that we are truly more than we appear; and at the same time, we appear as we are.

The paradox of form and energy and energy and form, for me, was no longer an intellectual curiosity, construct, or argument; it was simply a reality, a vibrant reality that continues to be active and is maintained in my spiritual heart center.

The difference it made in my life was simply in the area of insight, understanding, purification, and awareness. Another curtain had been pulled aside, and I was privy to a new dimension of reality. The ability to comprehend or believe no longer was a mystery.

Reverend Sandy learned the connection between form and energy. The awakening clarified the powerful energy at the base of her spine. Although the encounter, with the Lazarus rising, seemed sudden, she was ready and prepared.

A few years after my (Carla) initial transcendental realization in Lourdes, France, I had the beginning of the Lazarus rising. At the time I knew even less than Reverend Sandy did. When it began to rise, I had no idea what was happening or what it was called until I heard Jesus call it forth. It was then I became more cooperative.

February 1981

> I had just finished meditating. I got up and prepared for bed. My body hardly touched the bed when what felt like an electric current ran up from my lower back. Lying on my back, I did not have the slightest idea what was going on. I watched it. I hoped that it was not a physical problem.
>
> As the weeks passed, I began to get a clearer understanding from within. I became aware that it was a renewal process. I would hear from within, "I am the resurrection, I make all things new."
>
> I continued to rest in the awareness of my heart center area and allowed the current to have its way. The current raced up on each side of

my spine, and it shook my entire body. At first, the shaking was mild, but then it increased with almost a violent force. I remained passive, and I began to hear, "Rise, Lazarus, and come forth."

I became sure that this was part of my spiritual journey. It was Jesus Christ, through the Holy Spirit, calling forth a powerful energy to renew my entire being.

I continued to remain focused on the Lazarus rising as it moved within my being. It would start around four o'clock in the morning and last for about an hour and a half. I continued to hear, "Lazarus, rise and come forth."

The body shaking became much stronger, and the energy did not rise higher than my shoulder area. It felt like an earthquake. There was no physical pain, but it left me tired and at times totally exhausted.

I read the scripture passages about the Lazarus event as it happened in the Gospel (John 11:25–44), I was not able to grasp the inner meaning. Jesus was always saying something or doing something in scriptures that went beyond the apparent meaning. I prayed for a better understanding about what was going on and how it was related to the renewed life healing of the Lazarus rising by Jesus.

It was not until August that Jesus revealed that when we were ready, the dormant/sleeping (Lazarus) spiritual life energy force is quickened at the base of the spine and rises upward through spiritual centers to renew our entire structure.

It does this through the power and activity of the Holy Spirit in the name of Jesus so that we might enjoy the fullness of life in the Christ in the oneness of God.

An early afternoon in October, I laid down on my back on the bed to rest. I was suddenly startled with the sound of a firm, commanding voice, "Lazarus, rise and come forth." I had not heard it spoken so forcefully before.

The Lazarus rising moved in one smooth, ongoing, gentle motion up the center of my spine to the top of my head. It was a warm liquid flow. My entire body tenderly vibrated. My body felt as though it were rising two feet above the bed, and I heard singing. I could only recall the words, "Give thanks."

I realized a blissful, exhilarating state of being. The last words that I remembered saying before entering this state were, "Oh God." It was as though it was too much to bear.

I had thought that I could not change anymore, but I did! I no longer felt that there was anything or anyone missing in my life. It was sufficient to be in oneness with whom and what "I am." There was no one or thing outside of my being. All was a constant one, always one.

Unlike for Reverend Sandy, for me the Lazarus rising

awakening took nine months to run its course within me. Each of us progresses on our spiritual journey as we are ready and prepared along the straight and narrow path.

In November 1981 I attended a lecture on yoga. I learned something about what was called the kundalini and the seven chakras. The speaker discussed a dormant energy force and the necessity for being prepared for it to rise: "One must have a positive, receptive attitude." By this he meant not having a selfish motive and that the best preparation was through meditation, service, and love for others:

> I left the lecture that night thinking, how interesting it is that a Hindu has a renewal system that is similar to that of a Christian. Truly, there is but one God and only the language is different! The Holy Spirit, after all, does speak in many tongues.[1]

I found the Lazarus rising to be purifying, renewing, and transforming. It is wise to examine it in the context of your spiritual unfolding process.

If the Lazarus rising becomes active during your Christ Centered Prayer practice or when lying down and causes your body to shake uncontrollably, you may simply repeat, "God *is*, God *is*," until you feel relaxed and consciously in control again.

Consciously allow Jesus to bring forth the Lazarus rising.

---

1 Carla Mancari, *When Jesus Is the Guru: A Wayward Christian's Spiritual Walk* (Tucson: Wheatmark, 2010), 114.

Stay aware, but do not attempt to force the energy. If it should overwhelm you, stop and get up from your practice or resting. Work slowly with the Lazarus rising in your own time and at your own pace.

The Christ Centered Prayer practice, in time, allows the dormant energy to begin rising naturally. Once the energy has traversed the six centers and has reached the seventh center at the crown of your head, consciously return the energy to your Spiritual Heart Center area and maintain it there.

It is ill advised to use practices that would force the dormant energy to ascend. It may result in overtaxing the nervous system and perhaps causing bodily or psychological harm. It is best to respect the process and never force it.

The Christ Centered Prayer practice prepares the body and mind consciousness for the Lazarus rising. When you practice the Christ Centered Prayer and live a moral life in thought, word, and deed, the Lazarus rising is a subtle, natural occurrence (if necessary).

If you wish to have additional information, talk with a teacher. If you have a teacher, it is wise to seek guidance. Having an experienced teacher work with you is best. What is most important is that you are aware of what may take place and are receptive. However, stay aware; you are not alone. Jesus is your inner guide on this inner journey, and He holds you close.

The rising of the dormant energy helps cleanse the spiritual centers, purifying negativity. It also may pave the way for realizations to unfold. You have the stillness and silence to realize beyond the spiritual centers. No matter how exhilarating the Lazarus rising awakening is, it is not a be-all, end-all. The journey continues.

Thirteen

Wisdom

Slow to Rise

From the inner kingdom,
slow to rise …
wisdom.
– cm

WISDOM IS SLOW to rise; therefore, wisdom lags behind realizations. Wisdom does not necessarily come with age. It comes when you have been properly seasoned in living out from truth revealed and realized.

Wisdom has a way of rising well after insights, revelations, and realizations have occurred. It requires that you have patience and a close relationship with the inner silence to be available when wisdom chooses to make its presence known. However, it is well worth the wait.

When you have a realization, it does not mean you are instantly wise. Realizations require time to expand and deepen. Do the Christ Centered Prayer practice, rest in the awareness of your Spiritual Heart Center area, learn to hold your tongue, and wisdom will rise in its own time. "Be not wise in thine own eyes: fear the LORD, and depart from evil" (Prov. 3:7).

The Christ Centered Prayer practice may cause life changes. It is wise to live quietly with any life change. The mind, because of previous conditioning, is slow to acknowledge truth. An adjustment period may be necessary for the calm assurance of wisdom to rise. Because wisdom *is* slow to rise, ponder your realizations and live with them. Allow wisdom to surface in its own time, "Happy is the man that findeth wisdom and *that* getteth understanding" (Prov. 3:13).

Wisdom is not an acquisition, and it is not gleaned from acquired knowledge. It already exists. It is an inherent gift within all who awaken to the realization of God in Christ and the Christ in all. Say less, and turn your hearing inward to your Spiritual Heart Center where wisdom expresses through the Holy Spirit in the name of Jesus Christ.

You cannot dip into memories for wisdom. Wisdom's birth is a constant present. It is not a memory. Wisdom rises as you practice the Christ Centered Prayer and live out from your realizations, your God nature.

Reverend Sandy's recognition of wisdom took time and patience. She shares her delight in it:

> Perhaps there is a body wisdom so deep that it alleviates fear. I have a mind, senses, intellect, reason, emotional body and, whether or not I like it, an ego and sense of self. My wisdom has more pathways to traverse before coming to be second nature and ultimately first nature. Wisdom for me has taken time to recognize. I find it rises slowly from a deep place within my core and heart. Uncensored, it is an impulse that rises in purity and is translated in truth. The "I am" able to live wisely.
>
> Wisdom has come after the natural progression rising from realizations within the heart. This amalgam of impressions aligns in intelligent order and speaks a language called wisdom. It is a silent language yet powerful beyond measure. Rooted in wisdom the ebb and flow of life's contingencies are rendered manageable.
>
> I take neither credit nor offer apology for

> my wisdom or lack of. Wisdom simply is more or less operative in my life. As I journey further on this path toward wholeness in Christ through the power of the Holy Spirit, I find wisdom being quietly ingratiated in my every thought, feeling, emotion and action. Wherever I go, it goes. It is a sweet sound in my heart and the song it sings is the glory of God.[2]

Reverend Sandy found wisdom was a joy in her life. She realized wisdom was worth the wait. The taste of it delighted her life, and the recognition of it progressed her spiritual journey.

For me (Carla), wisdom allowed me to live through what seemed like an endless struggle before it rose with the necessary instruction that would ease my mind and soften my heart. I was determined not to accept Jesus the Christ in my life. He seemed too divine, too remote.

Jesus had become an impossible hurdle to get over on my quest for truth. I could not relate to this Jesus the Christ, Son of God, until wisdom instructed me to look in a different direction, one that I had not entertained. It was a connection with the personal Jesus who would help take me beyond the personal sense to the realized Jesus the Christ, from the human to the divine. Now why didn't I think of that? My mind had been much too cluttered with traditional religious conditioning:

2 Ibid., 211.

> During my spiritual journey, I constantly struggled with wanting to know God/truth. Not until I was first instructed to, "Find the man Jesus" did I understand the importance of connecting with the personal Jesus.
>
> I too, needed to know the Father/God with whom Jesus professed to be One. This was the God of all goodness and love, the Father/God within Jesus and within me; however, until I knew the personal Jesus, it was impossible to move beyond that point to the impersonal being and the awareness of God as Truth and Spirit.[3]

Wisdom guided me to pray the rosary. It was through contemplating and then mindfully praying each mystery of the rosary (joyful mysteries, sorrowful mysteries, and glorious mysteries) that the life of Mother Mary and the beginnings of Jesus were revealed, the baby, the youth, and the man.

Praying the rosary took me on an experience of the spiritual journey as none other. The rosary took me from the beginning of the recorded scriptural events of Mother Mary and her Son to the end of its promised beginning of an awakened life.

Praying the rosary allowed me to be with Mary when she was asked to conceive Jesus; to be with Jesus as He grew into manhood; and to travel with Him as He taught, was persecuted, was crucified, and was resurrected. I was beneath

---

3 Carla Mancari, *When Jesus Is the Guru: A Wayward Christian Woman's Spiritual Walk* (Tucson: Wheatmark, 2010), 59.

the cross with His Mother, when He asked John to care for her. I witnessed Jesus when He asked the Father to forgive them who crucified Him, and I felt the pain in a mother's heart when her Son died upon a cross. I was also there for the burial, resurrection, and ascension. "Ah, the rosary, the power and the glory of praying rosary!"[4]

All of this was given to me by wisdom's instruction to pray the rosary. You cannot put a price on wisdom. "The topaz of Ethiopia shall not equal it, neither shall it be valued with pure gold" (Job 29:19).

I soon realized that Jesus was like any other human being. He was flesh and blood. He was a baby totally dependent on His Mother. He had to learn to talk and to walk as all babies do. He was not a distant God to be worshiped but a friend, a trusted friend, who I wanted to follow:

> He wasn't just an impersonal Son of God; rather, He was also the Son of Mother Mary with all of the humanity that the rest of humankind possessed. He was real, flesh and blood. He was a human being like me and like you who walked the earth. Somehow, I thought, I too must follow Him, His Way. He had now become more than an inner guide. Jesus was my example, a model, a Way to be, a Way to follow, and a living presence.[5]

---

4 Sandra Casey-Martus and Carla Mancari, *The Lessons: How to Understand Spiritual Principles, Spiritual Activities, and Rising Emotions, Volume One* (Tucson: Wheatmark, 2008), 147-48.

5 Carla Mancari, *When Jesus Is the Guru: A Wayward Christian's Spiritual Walk,* (Tuscon: Wheatmark, 2010), 51.

I was so taken with the personal sense of Jesus that I trusted He would take me all of the way to the Christ of *my* being. All doubts faded, and I followed Him without hesitation.

Wisdom teaches that you will face times on this journey when you may need to slow down, to go back to basics. An overreach may bog you down. There are times for a need to ponder the little things on this journey before you can handle the big ones. You may be so immersed in your own humanity that being aware of that little babe who is usually celebrated and talked about during a Christmas season is not enough. That babe, with the help of His earthly, human mother and father, grew up in all of His humanity.

This babe had a significant human journey. Wisdom walked me through the mysteries of the rosary to reveal this human journey that I could relate to and identify. Jesus walked the Way, He lived the Way, and He became the Way.

Jesus always knows that what is true of Him, is true of you. The personal relationship with Jesus takes you to Jesus the Christ. Find the man Jesus. If you can do this, you will understand what Jesus meant when He instructed, "Then said Jesus unto his disciples, If any man will come after me, let him deny himself, and take up his cross, and follow me" (Matt. 16:24).

The importance of having a personal relationship with Jesus is a gift to be valued. As spiritual relationships (inner and outer) deepen and you become more aware of your continuous spiritual activities, spiritual maturity evolves in wisdom and contentment.

No, you are not wise to run before you can walk. Your struggle on your spiritual journey is with your humanity not your divinity. The Christ Centered Prayer practice wisely begins with care for your humanity by allowing you to practice in a comfortable position. It neither bends you out of shape nor demands long sittings. It is a gentle, soft practice from your humanity to your divinity.

Find the baby Jesus, the boy Jesus, the youth Jesus, the man Jesus, and you will find the humanity that connects you directly with Jesus. It is the connected humanity that may help take you to the realization of Jesus the Christ in all of *His* divinity and *yours*.

Fourteen

Christian

Lost, Found/Saved, and Disciple

A wanderer, you have been.
Going from place to place until …
silence called you to Him.
– cm

DO YOU WEAR the Christian label and yet journey on other non-Christian paths? Are you like the miner who is easily attracted to fool's gold? It may be shiny and look like the real thing, but the real thing it is not.

The Christ Centered Prayer gives you an opportunity to get in touch with your Christian roots. Constantly bouncing about between or among different meditation groups impedes your spiritual progress. It is much like picking up two sticks and rubbing them to get fire. If you constantly put them down to place your attention elsewhere, your fire will never be lit.

You may be a Christian wandering in the wilderness. You may want to believe you can find your Christian roots in any meditation tradition. You may be satisfied to fill your spiritual journey by seeking only a glimpse of what is in your own backyard. Confusion may set in when you attempt to place your feet in two or more different paths.

Christians fall into three major stages: lost, found/saved, or disciple. They may move about from one stage to another. It is, after all, a spiritual journey that consists of many doubts and temptations.

The Three Major Christian Stages:

1. Lost

A lost Christian is one who is determined to believe that any of the many different paths includes the straight gate and narrow way. It is the reason that a lost Christian may fail to find the straight gate and narrow way. "Because Strait is the gate, and narrow is the way, which leadeth unto life, and few there be that find it" (Matt. 7:14).

Because the Christian journey is a straight and narrow one, it is easy to be seduced and get lost on the many broad roads. "Enter ye in at the strait gate: for wide is the gate, and broad is the way that leadeth to destruction, and many there be which go in thereat" (Matt. 7:13).

A lost Christian invests time and effort in struggling to hold on to conditioned deceptions. That person may find it difficult to give up what has become the familiar and to surrender to the unknown. A lost Christian chooses a bunny trail, hopping about from one path to another. A lost Christian has a strong resistance to the straight gate and narrow way, and easily becomes annoyed by any suggested guidance to move in the direction of their Christian roots.

A lost Christian avoids the inward journey and instead wanders from one intellectual path to another. The easier part of a spiritual journey is to meander through different paths and teachings.

The many different intellectual teachings about the truth may stimulate the mind and cause a psychological high. There may be a constant rising to the mental states, and the mind tends to stay where *it* feels good. It is an emotional high, yes, but an emotional high is not the Christ reality. The intellectual chatter of this world may hold sway. ". . . the letter killeth, but the spirit giveth life" (2 Cor. 3:6).

Jesus does not accept the loss of even one of His own. Jesus perseveres until a lost Christian is safely where that Christian belongs. While a lost Christian may be seeking a teaching, Jesus is seeking the lost Christian. "What man of you, having an hundred sheep, if he lose one of them, doth not leave the ninety and nine in the wilderness, and go after that which is lost, until he find it?" (Luke 15:4).

The Christ Centered Prayer may bring you into the presence of the Jesus who asked His Father to grant to you the glory the Father had given Jesus. The Jesus who asks this, shares His divine nature with you. You cannot separate yourself from that with which you are. "And the glory which thou gavest me I have given them; that they may be one, even as we are one" (John 17:22).

On this long and difficult journey home, you may have walked many paths, traveled many roads, and climbed many mountains. Yet, the journey seems without end. Why not try Jesus? Why not say yes to Jesus, who never says no to you? Become a *found* Christian. Or is it more important to deny Jesus than to bend a knee and confess that you are in need of His shepherding? "And when the chief Shepherd shall appear, ye shall receive a crown of glory that fadeth not away" (1 Peter 5:4).

2. Found/Saved

The words *found* and *saved* in a Christian setting are much like the word *love*. They are often used and are open to a variety of interpretations and misinterpretations. The goal of a found/saved Christian is to come into the presence of the Holy Spirit in the name of Jesus Christ and to know the Father as Jesus knew Him. "I came forth from the Father, and am come into the world again, I leave the world, and go to the Father" (John 16:28).

A found/saved Christian's commitment is to awaken to

the good news that Jesus shared and that He was willing to be crucified for. Pride may steer a Christian in other directions. The arrogance of pride may prevent a found/saved Christian from being fully exposed to the teachings of Jesus Christ and have a close relationship with Him.

The Christ Centered Prayer puts a found/saved Christian in a position to receive the teachings of Jesus. It keeps a found/saved Christian's awareness where it belongs: on the Christ.

The Christ Centered Prayer reveals Jesus Christ as more than just a man who once walked the earth. The kingdom that He spoke of and the Father/God that He glorified are yours. "These things have I written unto you that believe on the name of the Son of God; that ye may know that ye have eternal life, and that ye may believe on the name of the Son of God" (1 John 5:13).

For a found/saved Christian, Jesus Christ is Lord, master, guru, and teacher. There is an acceptance of Jesus's invitation to become a disciple. "And he saith unto them, Follow me, and I will make you fishers of men" (Matt. 4:19).

3. Disciple

A Christian disciple is one who follows Jesus Christ and His teaching. As it is for Jesus, it is for all who would choose to be a disciple. Discipleship is the acceptance of the spiritual hand of the heavenly Father upon the disciple.

"And when he had found him [Saul] he brought him unto Antioch. And it came to pass, that a whole year they assembled themselves with the church, and taught much people. And the disciples were called Christians first in Antioch" (Acts 11:26).

A disciple of Jesus Christ is humble and firm, is grounded in uninterrupted truth, and knows always, "Ye are of God, little children, and have overcome them: because greater is he that is in you, than he that is in the world" (1 John 4:4).

There comes a moment in time on a spiritual journey when an invitation is presented to follow Jesus Christ, and *only* Jesus Christ. Jesus does not say to follow Him while you attempt to tag along on other paths. Following Jesus Christ on a singular path requires your full attention.

A divided house will fall, and a divided consciousness will struggle to maintain its place. A disciple selects one path and gives it his or her all. "And Jesus knew their thoughts, and said unto them, Every kingdom divided against itself is brought to desolation; and every city or house divided against itself shall not stand" (Matt. 12:25).

A disciple lives at a time and in a world where many choices are vying for attention. Jesus's call is one of the many choices. Jesus anoints, guides, and directs a disciple's footsteps along the way to the Father's house. There is no greater anointing, no greater discipleship. "But ye are a chosen generation, a royal priesthood, an holy nation, a peculiar people; that ye should shew forth the praises of him who hath called you out of darkness into his marvelous light" (1 Peter 2:9).

Whenever a disciple steps up to the plate in the name of Jesus Christ, the Holy Spirit may reveal that disciple's true nature. Trust the oneness of being and surrender to it so that it becomes as natural as breathing. A disciple has the necessary wherewithal to accomplish whatever the Holy Spirit requires. "Let your light so shine before men, that they may see your good works, and glorify your Father which is in heaven" (Matt. 5:16).

The confidence and ability to maintain a spiritual walk as a disciple of Jesus Christ is rooted squarely and firmly in the Christ consciousness. When the Christ Centered Prayer method is practiced, the unreal recedes and the truth, the real, may be revealed. Jesus is the way; a disciple need only follow. "And thine ears shall hear a word behind thee, saying This is the way, walk ye in it, when ye turn to the right hand, and when ye turn to the left" (Isa. 30:21).

A disciple of Jesus Christ is tempted. The appearances of this world do not give up. Temptations come in many different ways. A temptation wants what a disciple has (a realized consciousness) and will appear in any fashion necessary to get it. "For all that is in the world, the lust of the flesh, and the lust of the eyes, and the pride of life, is not of the Father, but is of the world" (1 John 2:16).

Accept a discipleship in humility, and surrender. It is natural for the conscious mind, for a time, to shake at the changing wonders that it must behold. A Christian discipleship manages the mind's doubts and hesitations. "For with God nothing shall be impossible" (Luke 1:37).

Did you recognize yourself in any of the Christian stages? There are many questions for you to ponder and many for you to answer. The Christ Centered Prayer may help you answer the question of which you are: lost, found/saved, or disciple.

Many Christians unintentionally take detours. It is the mind's work to want to take a simple truth and weave it into complex exercises and intellectual jargon. That is what the mind does best. It is easy to get lost in the world of opposites. "For many are called, but few are chosen" (Matt. 22:14).

Jesus perseveres and never gives up on you. There is an old spiritual principle that goes something like this: "When the student is ready, the teacher will appear." It has been proven to be true.

There is, however, another spiritual principle that I found to be true in my Christian service. It goes like this: "Jesus is always seeking *and* readying the student for the teacher to appear." Jesus is a model who you may follow, a model who gives to your life direction and guidance.

In the scriptures, Jesus lays out a pattern tailored and cut to fit each one of you. True, Jesus is not always the easiest model to follow, but what He asks of you, He asked even more of Himself. "For even the Son of man came not to be ministered unto, but to minister, and to give his life a ransom for many" (Mark 10:45).

Many religious models are out there to follow, imitate, or represent. As a Christian, what greater model could you have than Jesus? What greater model would you want? What greater discipleship is there? "Herein is my Father glorified, that ye bear much fruit; so shall ye be my disciples" (John 15:8).

Jesus models what He teaches. It is not, "Do as I say, not

as I do." Jesus laid down His life. What percentage of your time and energy are you willing to expend to follow Jesus? "Then said Jesus unto his disciples, If any man will come after me, let him deny himself, and take up his cross, and follow me" (Matt. 16:24).

Are you a Christian who fears stepping away from the old and moving on to the new? Are you a Christian who can say yes when Jesus calls. Will you take up your cross, yourself, and follow Jesus?

Reverend Sandy was given the opportunity to say yes to Jesus. It was not an easy yes. She struggled with all of the doubts and fears that come with stepping out in faith and trust:

> For about eleven years I was a retreat director and had been teaching Christian contemplative prayer under the auspices of an internationally respected, well-known, and credentialed organization. There were side benefits that came along with this relationship. As an obedient and well-schooled representative, I was able to fly under the wings of well-known, respected, and published authors on the spiritual journey. By virtue of the organization's respectability I was rendered "respectable."
>
> The work was mutually enriching for the individuals I taught and I have only gratitude for the guidance and support I have received. There is a lot to be said about such a relationship that is

noble and appropriate. Unfortunately, it also has its limitation. Understandably, I was to present faithfully the teachings as I had been taught. This I did. However, there were times toward the end of my tenure with this organization, when I deeply felt a desire to speak out of my own experience or add to a previously revealed teaching. The latitude for such speech did not lie within the established boundaries of the organization.

The commitment I made to faithfully present this teaching and the challenge to that which was coming from my internal integrity created quite a crisis of loyalty. I tried my hardest not to leave and had numerous heated conversations with my teacher about "why I needed to stay for reputation, respectability, and access." After all, "Who was I to speak? Who was I to presume I could speak with authority? Who would want to listen to Sandy?"

It just seemed ridiculous to even entertain such a step. I recall lamenting and arguing these issues and said to my teacher, "How can I teach these spiritual principles based on my experience? And what about footnotes? Who would I footnote? Myself?" My teacher's response would always be a soft "Yes."

The irony of my questions and her response was totally lost on me. It was inconceivable to me that a 57 year-old Episcopal woman priest, trying to make ends meet in the woods of Wyoming would have something to add to the deposit of knowledge catalogued by the Spanish Mystics and great theologians of our day.

It was beyond my wildest imagination. The thought of speaking in my own voice as a disciple of Jesus Christ was both compelling and terrifying. Nevertheless in spite of my protestations this was, in fact, laid before me. The directive was clear, "choose."

Immediately the temptations rose. My initial impulse was to refuse, retreat and forget that I ever entertained the possibility. After a week of emails between myself and my teacher, protesting such a move, appealing to institutional loyalty, commitment, and obligations, I had to face square on the real questions, 'Whom would I serve? To whom would I be faithful? Would I be willing to trust and serve the Christ of my being whose credentials were written in my heart and not on parchment?' If I said, "Yes" to that Master (Jesus) then I knew my life would never be the same again because it would no longer be my life.

In utter terror, with few notable credentials, no reservoir of celebrities, and absolutely no footnotes, I decided to follow the inner prompting of the Holy Spirit in the name of Jesus Christ and step out in faith and trust. I had no idea that the plethora of material and teaching found in these volumes [*The Lessons* and other books] would come forth as a result of that momentous decision.

> I thought I would have no books, no teaching, no method, no invitations to teach, no nothing. In fact, I have received everything and then some! As the woman giving birth with no previous knowledge of the gifts lavished by God on her child, I stand in awe of what is being brought forth into this world. And for that I can only give glory to God.[1]

Reverend Sandy's trust in Jesus's call was confirmed with abundance in all categories of her life. What she was asked to give up was paltry compared to what she received. "That thine alms may be in secret: and thy Father which seeth in secret himself shall reward thee openly" (Matt. 6:4).

Lost, found, or disciple—which are you? It is easy to get lost, a joy to be found, and an awakening to be a disciple. The Christ Centered Prayer method invites you to come listen to Jesus. Come follow Him, come walk with Him, and come talk with Him. No middle man, no word, no mantra is necessary. He awaits the sound of *your* voice. Listen for His. "That at the name of Jesus every knee should bow, of things in heaven, and things under the earth" (Phil. 2:10).

---

1 Sandra Casey-Martus and Carla Mancari, *The Lessons: How to Understand Spiritual Principles, Spiritual Activities, and Rising Emotions, Volume One* (Tucson: Wheatmark, 2008), 66–67.

Fifteen

Additional Prayer Practices

Staying Grounded

He, who a thousand did feed,
meets, in the moment, your need.
– cm

FROM THE CHRIST Centered Prayer revelation comes six additional prayer practices to help you with the Christ Centered Prayer method and your adjustment to living a balanced life. These six additional prayer practices may also help you with any of the contents discussed in chapter 7.

Jesus gives you the necessary help to move you on your spiritual journey as smoothly as possible. When practiced as needed, these prayer practices may promote stability and balance in your spiritual awakening progress.

The Six Additional Prayer Practices:

1. The Power Prayer: A and B

The power prayer is a dialogue practice that may allow you to address a particularly difficult mental issue that rises repeatedly in your mind states of consciousness. It is its own unique dialogue prayer method and is to be used in the short term *only* when necessary.

"Its sole purpose is to remove invested power in a specific emotionally charged situation. It does not replace your twice-daily silent Christ Centered Prayer practice. Also, the power prayer practice is never to be mixed with your Christ Centered Prayer practice."[1]

Emotional, tormenting rising thoughts are conditioned responses. You may experience them as a positive or negative solid steel forms that seem impenetrable. Because you have previously given the emotional, tormenting rising

1 Ibid, 23.

thoughts power, having accepted a false belief in them, even attempting to make the least dent may be a huge struggle.

However, that which appears as strong as steel may bend to your will and melt in the furnace of the realization that a conditioned sense impression has only the power you give it. You are a spiritual being created in the image your God source.

You may practice the power prayer in two ways: sitting or as you go about your daily activities. When practicing either way, it is most important to remember the immediacy of responding, "No power; God is."

The "No power" is your recognition that the tormenting thought of itself has no power. The "God is" acknowledges that only God *is* and right there in the moment of the tormenting thought's rising, God alone exists.

(A) The Power Prayer, Sitting Practice:

» Sit comfortably with your eyes closed. When the tormenting thought rises, immediately, silently, and with conviction think, *"No power; God is."*

» Become aware of your Spiritual Heart Center area, and rest in awareness.

» Each time the tormenting thought rises, immediately repeat, *"No power; God is."* The length of sitting time you practice power prayer A is optional.

(B) The Power Prayer, Daily Activities Practice:

» When a tormenting thought rises during your daily activities, silently repeat, "No power; God is" as often as is necessary.

- » Immediately refocus your attention to the outer activity.
- » You do *not* bring your awareness to your Spiritual Heart Center area.

The power prayer (A or B or both) may bring you into a neutral zone of non-responding and restore your inner peace. It may activate the forgiveness, purification, and the holy instant process (chapter 5). All may be accomplished in the Spiritual Heart Center by the Holy Spirit in the name of Jesus Christ.

Never practice either power prayer methods while driving or operating any kind of mechanical equipment. Do not practice any prayer method or meditation in your parked car and then immediately drive. Always be sure you are fully alert before driving. Whenever your safety is at issue, *do not* practice *any* prayer method or meditation.

2. The Hand-to-Heart Prayer

The hand-to-heart prayer method is to be practiced in a spiritual energy crisis or at a time of needed guidance. As you practice the Christ Centered Prayer, many inner changes may begin to occur. An expansive consciousness creates times of highs and lows. At times your energy may vibrate so rapidly that you feel as if you are on a roller coaster.

You may not understand what is happening, and if immediate help is not available, the silent hand-to-heart prayer may be a short-term solution. This prayer method may be practiced anywhere, in any position, and during any activity that does *not* involve your safety.

The Hand-to-Heart Prayer Practice:

- » Place your hand over the Spiritual Heart Center area (center of chest between the breasts).
- » Take a long, deep breath, and exhale slowly, relaxing your mind and body.
- » Rest your attention on your hand in the silence of awareness. If necessary, repeat step two several times.

The silent hand-to-heart prayer practice may help bring immediate calm and restore your vibrating energy's balance. Do not let the simplicity of the hand-to-heart prayer practice fool you. Many times Jesus used His hands to heal, bless, or still the waters. The Holy Spirit in the name of Jesus Christ empowers the hand-to-heart prayer.

3. The Listening-In Prayer

The Christ Centered Prayer is constantly guiding you within to your Spiritual Heart Center. The listening-in prayer method may allow you to come to hear the silent, sacred language of God that you may come to understand more easily than any language of this world. "It is the spirit that quickeneth; the flesh profiteth nothing: the words that I speak unto you, *they* are spirit, and *they* are life" (John 6:63).

The Listening-In Prayer Practice:

- » Sit, take a long deep breath, slowly exhale, and relax. Turn your hearing inward toward the awareness of your Spiritual Heart Center area (center of chest, between the breasts).

- » Softly listen in as though you were waiting for a phone to ring.
- » Listen to the silence. Be patient and quiet for a few minutes. Then go about your outer business.

The silent space you visit in awareness reveals whatever it is you need at the moment. The listening-in prayer is a separate silent prayer practice. It is not to be mixed with your Christ Centered Prayer practice.

Reverend Sandy was drawn to the understanding that as a priest, she needed something greater than herself. She realized she needed the silence that could only be realized within her Spiritual Heart Center:

> As a priest, I was aware that I had to be realized. It didn't matter how many courses I had taken or how many books I had read, I also knew that heaven could not be taken by force. This was going to take time. I could not possibly have a ready answer for all the questions put to me.
>
> After many years of prayer and the faithful practice of listening-in, I found answers to questions rose quite effortlessly. My mother always told me to think before I spoke, but I have come to a deeper understanding. I must "listen" before I speak. This has proven to be invaluable.[2]

2 Ibid., 124–125.

Reverend Sandy was aware that books could not hold the answers to the many questions that she would be faced with in her priestly ministry. The listening-in prayer gave her the assurance she needed when working with others.

The listening-in prayer may also benefit and improve relationships with family and friends. During a listening-in prayer practice, your inner silent hearing may deepen.

You may find a clarity of perception in the discernment of conflicting points of view. Discernment rises with compassion and brings a quick resolution to a present moment's need. Discernment thrives in a listening-in environment.

Mary, found that the listening-in prayer practice served her well in her relationship with her mother. She learned to listen-in, which dispelled the fear of inadequacy she commonly felt while visiting her mother:

> The practice of listening-in has transformed my relationship with my mother. I would frequently hear in our conversation, the hint of "I'm not good enough, I should be a better daughter." I don't know if my mother was conveying those messages or if I were just making them up in my own mind.
>
> One day my aging mother was telling me about her friend, who had hurt her hip and had to

> use a walker. Her daughter was taking care of the lawn chores for her mother.
>
> As my mother was telling me this, I felt the typical "I am not a good daughter, I should be mowing my mother's lawn." I started listening-in and the conversation transformed. I realized that my mother was simply telling me about her friend and how happy she was for her because her daughter was able to help her.
>
> The conversation had nothing to do with me, and my mother was not hinting that she wanted me to mow her lawn. Instead of feeling inadequate and having hurt feelings, I, for the first time, really heard my mother. I too could feel happy for her friend and the help she was getting from her daughter.
>
> From that time on, when talking to my mom, I always listen-in. I don't get defensive and whenever the feeling of being an inadequate daughter rises, I simply go back to listening-in. I have found a deep love for my mother that had previously been supplanted by false sense of not being good enough.[3]

Mary's listening-in prayer practice gave her the tool that she needed. It was practical in her daily outer activity. It improved her relationship with her mother and freed her from self-condemnation.

3 Printed with letter of permission.

While listening-in to the inner silence within your Spiritual Heart Center, you may find there is a silent, sacred language that speaks to you. The silent voice of God may rise. "The tongue of the wise useth knowledge aright: but the mouth of fools poureth out foolishness" (Prov. 15:2).

In the silence of your Spiritual Heart Center, there is an openness that is rooted in the bedrock of God's abiding presence. As you practice the listening-in prayer, the inner silence deepens. Answers to the questions or the solutions you seek may manifest through individuals, situations, objects, or whatever is necessary.

"The Holy Spirit in the name of Jesus is always communicating with you. Listen-in and you may hear. 'Who hath ears to hear, let him hear' (Matt. 13:9)."[1]

4. The Temptation Prayer

The temptation prayer is a silent, mental sword that gives you the power to cut to the quick temptations in their conceptual stage.

Temptations want what you have (a realized consciousness). If given the opportunity, they will trample all over your insights, revelations, and realizations. It is when you are comfortable with your spiritual progress that temptations may rise and come at you in the fiercest ways possible.

The further along you are on your spiritual journey, the more intense temptations become. And they never cease. They will use any means and seem to have a life of their own. After God had affirmed that Jesus was His beloved

---

1 Sandra Casey-Martus and Carla Mancari, *Your "Other Heart": The Best-Kept Secret* (Tucson: Wheatmark, 2010), 127.

Son, Jesus was tempted in the wilderness. "THEN was Jesus led up of the Spirit into the wilderness to be tempted of the devil" (Matt. 4:1).

Temptations never desist. Right up to your passing, a temptation will rise to play with your mind. "And at the ninth hour Jesus cried with a loud voice, saying, El-o-i, El-o-i, la-ma sa-bach tha-ni? Which is, being interpreted, "My God, my God, why has thou forsaken me?" (Mark 15:34).

Temptations are seducers that invite you to betray the Christ of your being. Strive to be more like the seed that fell upon the good ground. "But that on the good ground are they, which in an honest and good heart, having heard the word, keep it, and bring forth fruit with patience" (Luke 8:15).

Once grounded in truth, you have the upper hand. You have the strength not only to refuse a temptation's offer, but to grow stronger in conscious awareness of temptations.

Scripture offers guidance that may provide armor against the arrows of the tempter in all its disguises. It does not matter if a temptation appears as a person, situation, friend, or foe. The temptation prayer practice is the same.

The Temptation Prayer Practice:

» Stay alert to the possibilities of a rising temptation.
» When a temptation rises, mentally, silently say, "Get thee behind me, Satan."
» Silently, mentally repeat the phrase as often as the temptation rises. Do not dialogue or mentally engage with the rising temptation. A temptation thrives on chatter.

Being a disciple of Jesus Christ is an invitation for temptations to rise. The more you resist, the stronger and more insistent temptations become. They feed on your strength. Do not be fooled by what temptations may present. They may come at you with very appealing offers. It is the work of a temptation to make you an offer difficult to overcome.

5. The Healing Prayer

Many well-known shrines around the world (France, Portugal, and Mexico City are a few) are dedicated to the Blessed Mother Mary. Many individuals have visited these shrines and have found the guidance, comfort, healing, and peace they sought.

Blessed Mother Mary is a guide and a healer. When there is a physical or emotional need, Blessed Mother Mary's healing prayer may heal and comfort.

The Healing Prayer Practice:

» Lie down on your back and close your eyes. Place one hand on your Spiritual Heart Center area (chest, between the breasts) and your other hand on your abdomen.

» Take a long, deep inhalation breath, and slowly exhale. Relax your entire body and mind. Let go of all thoughts, plans, and expectations.

» Slowly and contemplatively listen to every word as you say three Hail Marys and one Glory Be.

Rest and trust in knowing that you are in the arms of Mother Mary and that she may heal and comfort a broken heart or a broken body.

You may rise from your rest whenever you wish. Rise slowly and allow yourself to become fully alert before moving about. There is no required time. Relax, let go, and trust Mother Mary. These are the only requirements.

You may receive the opposite of that which you expected. Your life may have secret places that are more broken than the obvious. Healing and comfort may not always manifest as you wish.

You may have times when an emotional healing is more necessary in your life than a physical one. It is important that you trust Mother Mary. As it is with Jesus, Mother Mary's guidance is always in the best interest of your welfare.

6. The Scripture Prayer

The scriptures hold within each word the sacredness of your journey. The scripture prayer is a practice of praying the Christian scriptures. The Christian scriptures contain the entire spiritual journey that leads to the oneness in awareness of your being.

The scriptures walk with you every step of the way from Genesis to Revelations. The Christian scriptures (New Testament) are the teachings of Jesus Christ. The scriptures are multileveled. They express themselves at a literal, metaphysical, and mystical level.

There are many states, frequencies of individual expressions of consciousness. Each individual expression of consciousness brings to the scriptures its level of consciousness that enables it to receive at its level of need.

Form the habit of listening-in to whatever scripture you have chosen. As your consciousness changes, so may the translations of the scriptures.

The Scripture Prayer Practice:

» Choose any scripture word, sentence, or verse. Read slowly and contemplatively.
» Bring your attention to your Spiritual Heart Center area and softly, quietly listen-in to the silence.
» Sit and allow whatever you are seeking to understand to rise. Allow the thoughts of Jesus's teaching to rise, and the mind will translate.

The scripture prayer practice is an active prayer practice. It is very helpful in opening up the depth and breadth of Holy Scripture to your conscious awareness.

Do not drift into the rising thoughts of the mind. Be patient. You cannot rush the practice. Pray the Scriptures a few minutes as often as you like. Do not attempt to figure out mentally the scripture's meaning. Always return to your Spiritual Heart Center area and again listen-in to the silence.

Praying the Christian scriptures may enhance your Christ Centered Prayer practice and progress on your spiritual journey. When you prepare yourself and are ready to receive scripture revelations, nothing in the scriptures will be denied.

You have been gifted with six additional helpful prayer practices. Use them in gratitude as often as necessary, and they will serve you well.

Sixteen

The Prodigal Son

Ten Steps

You are not alone.
The prodigal son comes home.
It is the same journey you are on.
– cm

THE CHRIST CENTERED Prayer practice guides you on a spiritual journey in awareness by the grace of the Holy Spirit in the name of Jesus Christ. The parable of the prodigal son summarizes, in ten steps, your entire spiritual journey.

The spiritual journey is an inward pilgrimage from the unknown to the known presence of God awareness. It is your journey home. You are not unlike the prodigal child returning home to your Father's house.

Reverend Sandy explains her understanding of the scripture's prodigal son parable. She points out the similarity of our spiritual journey:

> The Prodigal Son made a return journey from enmeshment in the world of illusion, and so do we. We move from a sense of separation and the separate sense of self to the realization of Oneness. This is the journey from ignorance, alienation, and suffering to awareness and, ultimately, from death to life.
>
> We come to realize that this "Word" of life and light exist within us. It is us, from all eternity, and it is the greatest gift the Father can give the Son, who shares all with us through the power of the Holy Spirit. To realize this gift gives glory, worship, and honor to God through the Holy Spirit in the name of Jesus Christ.[1]

1 Ibid., 10.

Reverend Sandy expresses that the "Word" of life is the greatest gift that the Father can give Jesus. It is this gift that the Son shares to awaken us to reality.

The Ten Prodigal Son's Spiritual Journey Steps:

Step 1. Temptation rises for you to leave your Father's kingdom/house (consciousness). "And he said, A certain man had two sons: And the younger of them said to his father, Father, give me the portion of goods that falleth to me. And he divided unto them his living" (Luke 15:11–12).

Step 2. You succumb to the temptation. Your state of consciousness changes as you enter the plane of opposites. The individual mind rises, and a personal sense of separation from your God being takes you on an imaginary, distant journey in consciousness away from your immortal life in the oneness of God. "And not many days after the younger son gathered all together, and took his journey into a far country, and there wasted his substance with riotous living. And when he had spent all, there arose a mighty famine in that land; and he began to be in want" (Luke 15:13–14).

Step 3. Your struggle and suffering begin in a world of opposites as you seek your help in the outer world of appearances. You become attached to persons and things. A false sense of a separate person has created the belief that you must make it on your own. "And he went and joined himself to a citizen of that country; and he sent him into his fields to feed swine. And he would fain have filled his belly with the husks that the swine did eat: and no man gave unto him" (Luke 15:15–16).

Step 4. You begin to wonder if there is not a better way to live. You feel an inner tug, a reminder of what you may have had before the world was. "And when he came to himself, he said, How many hired servants of my father's have bread enough and to spare, and I perish with hunger!" (Luke 15:17).

Step 5. You are ready to rise in consciousness, turn within, practice a silent prayer, and walk the straight gate and narrow path back to your Father's kingdom/house (consciousness). "I will arise and go to my father, and will say unto him, Father, I have sinned against heaven, and before thee, And am no more worthy to be called thy son: make me as one of thy hired servants" (Luke 15:18–19).

Step 6. As you turn within and practice the Christ Centered Prayer, the forgiveness-purification process begins. All that is necessary—scriptures, sacraments, books, and teachers—appear to support you on your inner journey. The Holy Spirit in the name of Jesus Christ is quick to come forth to meet you on the path and gently, quietly teach you all that Jesus promised. "And he arose, and came to his father. But when he was yet a great way off, his father saw him, and had compassion, and ran, and fell on his neck, and kissed him. And the son said unto him, Father, I have sinned against heaven, and in thy sight, and am no more worthy to be called thy son" (Luke 15:20–21).

Step 7. The doubts and a personal sense of separation begin to fade. You have overcome this world through forgiveness-purification. "But the father said to his servants,

Bring forth the best robe, and put it on him; and put a ring on his hand, and shoes on his feet: And bring hither the fatted calf, and kill it; and let us eat, and be merry" (Luke 15:22–23).

Step 8. Gradually you may begin to have insights, revelations, and realizations. You are home—the kingdom. You have realized your God being. "For this my son was dead, and is alive again; he was lost, and is found. And they began to be merry" (Luke 15:24).

Step 9. Others may be quick to question this thing you call truth. Others may question your worthiness. "And he [the older son] answering said to his father, Lo, these many years do I serve thee, neither transgress I at any time thy commandment: and yet thou never gavest me a kid, that I might make merry with my friends: But as soon as this thy son was come, which hath devoured thy living with harlots, thou hast killed for him the fatted calf" (Luke 15:29–30).

Step 10. Your awareness expands as wisdom rises, and you seek to maintain a balance between the inner and outer expressions of your reality. You fully awaken to your immortal, impersonal being in awareness. You are where you never left in the awareness of your being. "It was meet that we should make merry, and be glad: for this thy brother was dead, and is alive again; and was lost, and is found" (Luke 15:32).

The prodigal son had enough of the pain and suffering of the world. He wanted the safety and peace of his father's house.

The peace that ends wars between minds and bodies, individuals and nations, does not last. Great wars have been fought, and continue to be fought, to attain a lasting peace. Such a peace is a fading one and cannot be sustained.

Safety and peace come from a resting silence within your being. The deeper the silence, the greater the peace. An inner peace of your being is realized as you rest in the silence of your Spiritual Heart Center. It is a peace beyond the mind's intellect. Jesus often said, "Peace be with you." In His presence, peace is realized.

During the Christ Centered Prayer practice, as doubts cease to rise, you are no longer at war with your mind or body. In the spirit of your life, there are no battles to be waged or wars to be won. "The LORD will give strength unto his people; the LORD will bless his people with peace" (Ps. 29:11).

The peace that the prodigal son sought, and that you seek, is an all-pervasive one that reflects a calm, tranquil presence. It is beyond the understanding of this world. "And the peace of God, which passeth all understanding, shall keep your hearts and minds through Christ Jesus" (Phil. 4:7).

The prodigal son believed happiness could be found apart from his father's embrace. Happiness is a state that you usually seek within the environment from objects and other individuals. Such happiness may go as quickly as it comes because it is highly emotional, fickle, and unstable.

As you practice the Christ Centered Prayer, your seeking and longing for God may come to fruition, and you may find yourself in a natural place of contentment. It is an abiding state of grace. It is just there: immovable and steady. You are content. "But godliness with contentment is great gain. For we brought nothing into this world, and it is certain we can carry nothing out" (1 Tim. 6:6–7).

Contentment is a state of grace that allows you to live a balanced life. Others will ask you, "Are you happy?" You will find your response is always "I am content." You realize the peace that only the Holy Spirit in the name of Jesus Christ can give. You are in the moment, and you are contented. "Not that I speak in respect of want: for I have learned, in whatsoever state I am, therewith to be content" (Phil. 4:11).

Eternal life, hope, love, and faith are not in the past or future. They are in the unobstructed present. They always are. Do not look for a future event. It does not exist. Do not reminisce about days gone by. They no longer exist. *Now* is the necessary time and place, and you are here.

Like the prodigal son, turn toward your Father's house (kingdom). Turn within, turn within. Awaken to your reality. "Behold, I stand at the door, and knock: if any man hear my voice, and open the door, I will come in to him and will sup with him, and he with me." (Rev. 3:20). Won't you open it?

Seventeen

Cause and Effect

As You Sow, You Shall Reap!

Purified wrongs
bring an end to
comings and goings.
– cm

CAUSE AND EFFECT—AS you sow, you shall reap (known in the East as Karma)—is an operating law on this plane of opposites. It is a reaction to your every action, positive or negative.

Cause and effect insures descending and ascending (known in the East as reincarnation). Until all misuse of energy in thought, word, and deed is purified (chapter 5) the journey continues. "Be not deceived; God is not mocked: for whatsoever a man soweth, that also he shall reap" (Gal. 6:7).

Christians are fortunate in that scripture teaches it does not require lifetimes to overcome the law of cause and effect. In this lifetime, you can overcome and break the chains that bind. "Come now, and let us reason together, saith the LORD: though your sins be as scarlet, they shall be white as snow; though they be red like crimson, they shall be as wool" (Isa. 1:18).

Jesus did not fear death because He realized life eternal. He had come into this world and overcame it. "In the world ye shall have tribulation: but be of good cheer; I have overcome the world" (John 16:33).

Jesus realized His reality in the oneness of His Father—God—and taught that you, too, could do the same. "He that overcometh, the same shall be clothed in white raiment; and I will not blot out his name out of the book of life, but I will confess his name before my Father, and before his angles" (Rev. 3:5).

You may detach from the cycle of cause and effect by practicing the Christ Centered Prayer. Doing this allows forgiveness, purification, the holy instant (chapter 5), and detachment realization (chapter 11) to help you, like Jesus, overcome this world. "Him that overcometh will I make a pillar in the temple of my God, and he shall go no more out: and I will write upon him the name of my God" (Rev. 3:12).

It matters not if you believe in reincarnation. It is *this* lifetime that is the most important. It is *now* that you may awaken to the Christ of your being.

Turn within, practice the Christ Centered Prayer, and you too may recognize the Christ, as did the thief hanging next to Jesus. "And Jesus said unto him, Verily I say unto thee. To day shalt thou be with me in paradise" (Luke 23:43).

When all is said and the work is done—lessons learned, detachment realized, and energy purified—you will have accomplished overcoming this world. Your journey upon this plane of opposites will be finished. Reincarnation will no longer exist. You will have ascended beyond its reach. You will have come home to Jesus's and your Father's kingdom. Welcome home!

Eighteen

An Awakened Being

"Now What?"

"Strait is the gate and
narrow is the way."
Tested and tried . . .
your Sabbath has arrived.
– cm

THE CHRIST CENTERED Prayer promises nothing but may deliver all. It may deliver the Christ awakening that you long for. The problem is, what do you do with it?

You may have soared to the heights of your reality, and still you question, "Lord, here I am, your image, your light, and your way upon an earth of quicksand; now what?"

You have finally gone beyond this world of make-believe. You have done all the necessary spiritual practices, learned all the necessary lessons, you *are* the necessary enlightenment, and still you may be left befuddled about where, what, and how you will live your life in this world.

All your work, all your struggle has finally paid off big time. You are an awakened being, ready and willing to leave this plane of opposites. Yet, here you are still among the sleepwalkers, dream makers. Questions rise rapidly. You question yourself in reflection, "Did I think the world and its illusions of false concepts would disappear? Or did I think I would disappear?" Neither may happen. Instead, you are here, not of this world, but still in it. So, there may be a period of adjustment. Remember, wisdom is slow to rise.

All of your emotions are intact. All of your needs are met. All of the things of this world are at your disposal. You desire nothing, you have everything. You are a contemplative among a world of sleepwalkers and truth seekers. You know the truth, and yet you may find yourself still in a world of illusion, a world you no longer call home. "Now what?" Where to go from here?" "What do you do, and how do you do it?"

Your first thought may be to hide in a cave or remote

area away from the hustle and bustle of this world. Perhaps for a time you may be able to do just that, and it may be the wise thing to do, live in the silence and solitude with your realization of who and what you are. You may find, like most enlightened beings, you are called back into the thick of this world's activities.

At first, you may honestly put up a good fight, not wanting to be bothered by the time-illusions created by false concepts, wanting to stay at the zenith of your aware being. You may find yourself slowly or abruptly dragged back into the center of it all. If you have a teacher, you are wise to continue to work closely with him or her. A teacher will assist you to adjust to living between two worlds as smoothly as possible.

The "Now what?" does not have to be earth-shattering to be effective. Your work is to maintain your awakened state to the truth of your reality. You continue to practice the Christ Centered Prayer twice daily. You live quietly among the noise of this world. You are the expression of unconditional love, God's nature existing among those who struggle with doubts and temptations to the contrary. You serve and do what is necessary in each and every moment.

You may or may not teach others. You may or may not be called upon to guide another to the place you are in. The "What now?" is your light in the darkness that may brighten someone's life, stir an awakened moment, or plant a fruitful spiritual seed. Your very presence among the many, who are the one, is a light you cannot hide, nor should you.

Although you continue to walk in the dream, you are no longer a dreamer. Although you are aware of the false appearances, concepts, and illusions, you are no longer creating them. Through the Holy Spirit in the name of Jesus Christ, you are here as a witness to all who see you see the Father.

Now you are as you were in the beginning, in God, before the world existed. Now you are an awakened being. "Now what?" There is no "what," there is only the "now."

"Now," you are the living scriptures revealed in the lives of all you may see, pass, or touch. Like Jesus, you are a walking messenger creating the Father's footprints on this earth.[1]

---

1 Sandra Casey-Martus and Carla Mancari, *The Lessons: How to Understand Spiritual Principle, Spiritual Activities, and Rising Emotions, Volume One* (Tucson: Wheatmark, 2008), 225.

Summary

"And this is life eternal, that they might know thee the only true God, and Jesus Christ, whom thou hast sent" (John 17:3).

YOU ARE NOT the body. You are not the mind. You are not the senses. You are not the emotions. You are an aware conscious spiritual being *using* and *experiencing* a mind, a body, senses, and emotions.

Your spiritual journey is through the direct invitation and inner guidance of Jesus Christ. As you practice the Christ Centered Prayer, the straight gate and narrow way, the Holy Spirit in the name of Jesus Christ, the saints, and all previous realized individuals are walking every step of the way with you. You are truly a member in the community of saints!

Jesus is more often than not thought of as an unreachable spiritual being, one whom you may implore, to whom you may pray, and from whom you may beg forgiveness. All this you may do; however, the most important message this book, *The Christ Centered Prayer – Revelation: The Strait Gate and Narrow Way*, imparts about Jesus Christ is that with the Christ Centered Prayer practice, you may realize His presence. The distance between you and Jesus is imaginary. "Jesus Christ the same yesterday, and today, and for ever" (Heb. 13:8).

Jesus Christ is alive and well. He is a certainty, a living being with whom you may meet and embrace during your lifetime upon this earth plane. Unfortunately people may spend more time dwelling on Jesus's death than on His life. His death teaches you that He lived. His life teaches you that *you* live. "Yet a little while, and the world seeth me no more; but ye see me: because I live, ye shall live also" (John 14:19).

You may have the mistaken belief that you must die and go to heaven to meet Jesus. Truth, heaven, Jesus, and the

Father exist within you, and you may enter that kingdom. Through the Holy Spirit in the name of Jesus Christ, the kingdom of heaven and the presence of Jesus Christ are always yours, free and clear. No one can take you there. No one can give it to you. No one can sell it to you. No one can take it away from you. "For through him we both have access by one Spirit unto the Father" (Eph. 2:18).

Jesus's crucifixion was a necessary one-time event; but resurrection and ascension are an ongoing celebration of His and your life eternal. Jesus Christ is not a myth, an image, or an idol. Jesus is as real now as He ever was or will be. At no time does Jesus not stand and await your return to His and the Father's warm welcome home. "At that day ye shall know that I am in my Father, and ye in me, and I in you" (John 14:20).

Mystery or symbolic rituals need not surround Jesus's availability. The silent Christ Centered Prayer method, the straight gate and narrow way, may take you directly to His presence in the Spiritual Heart Center within you.

When Jesus walked the earth plane, He walked and talked directly to the Father within His being. Jesus came to teach you that you could do the same. The Father and Jesus are one, and your reality exists within that oneness. "That they all may be one; as thou, Father, art in me, and I in thee, that they also may be one in us: that the world may believe that thou hast sent me" (John 17:21).

You do not have to travel, pay large sums of money, perform mysterious rituals, or undergo difficult initiations. Learn the Christ Centered Prayer method. Turn within. Your Spiritual Heart Center will open to the presence and reality of the kingdom of God and Jesus Christ. Turn within and you are there, the place you never left and will always be.

Come home to the source of your reality without ever taking one step in any direction. Come home to where you existed before your birth and will after your death. "The Kingdom of God cometh not with observation: Neither shall they say, Lo here! Or, lo there! for, behold, the Kingdom of God is within you" (Luke 17:20–21).

The Christ Centered Prayer method brings a greater dimension to your daily practical outer living. As the practice accompanies you on your spiritual walk, knowing and trusting Jesus Christ adds the necessary clarity, understanding, and guidance to your life. "Trust in the LORD with all thine heart; and lean not unto thine own understanding. In all thy ways acknowledge him, and he shall direct thy paths" (Prov. 3:5–6).

Being a realized awakened individual is not something one wears as a badge of honor. It carries with it a multitude of responsibilities. A realized being is an aware light of an individual expression of the Christ. The Christ Centered Prayer practice may connect you in the oneness of your inner teacher and, if necessary, attracts an outer one. "When the student is ready, the teacher will appear" is a truism.

The journey will be whatever you make of it. If you struggle, it will be difficult. Surrender obediently to the Christ of your being. When you are devoted, with a determine purpose, to your Christ Centered Prayer practice, the journey may progress unobstructed until you are a fully realized, awakened being.

In a fully realized state of aware being, you come to

know the oneness of God's existence. The Holy Spirit transforms the normal mundane sleeper into the most magnificent, natural, and normal being—natural, because you are more comfortable with your physical sense form.

You have created the dream and the dreamer, neither of which is reality. You have identified with the dreamer and the dream; wake up and dream no more. Realize your reality. Doing this allows you to recognize the illusionary world of opposites and dissolves the false ties of self-identification to an imaginary life. "Lay not up for yourselves treasures upon earth, where moth and rust doth corrupt, and where thieves break through and steal" (Matt. 6:19).

You are comfortable and contented when you wake up to that which you are by divine gift, a beloved child of God. You are a spiritual being and always have been. Now is your time to discover reality. Discover your life in Christ that you possess and possesses you. Wake up.

We cannot promise you anything because the realized awakened state is not ours to give. We can only share the Christ Centered Prayer method with you and wish you a speedy, safe journey, an awakened state in the Christ of your be-ing, and the reality of your life.

Charts

Major Points

Review

Exercises

Practice, Ponder

Hearts in Triangles

Within, Without

Chart One: Major Points

Review

Wake Up and Dream Walk No More:

1. Attachments cause suffering.
2. The entire universe is consciousness.
3. You are an aware, free being. Wake up and live!
4. There is one Void God, one aware consciousness.
5. The one becomes the many. The many returns to the one.
6. This world, plane of opposites, is not your permanent home.
7. You are not that which you can taste, touch, smell, hear, feel, or think.
8. All that consciousness creates in the universe is relative to the universe.
9. You are not the mind, a person, or anything in the universe. You are not in the universe; the universe is in you. Yours is a greater reality.
10. You may be aware of being conscious, but you cannot be conscious of awareness.

11. **All in this world must deteriorate and die. The life you are is immortal, eternal.**
12. **With the help of the Christ Centered Prayer method, you may become aware of your Spiritual Heart Center and the Holy Spirit in the name of Jesus Christ.**
13. **Turn within to your Spiritual Heart Center and become aware of the spiritual guidance directing your spiritual progress and practical living.**
14. **Jesus the Christ is alive and well. Enter by the straight gate and narrow way, and know Him as He** *is* **and you** *are.*

Chart Two: Exercises

Practice, Ponder

1. *Attention*

Place your thumb and index finger together. Consciously focus your attention on the thumb touching the index finger, and then shift your attention to the index finger touching the thumb.

2. *Beyond Differences*

For one day, do any household chore as though it were a sacred ritual.

3. *Expanding Conscious Awareness*

Sitting on a chair, close your eyes and be aware of your bottom touching the chair seat, the chair feet touching the floor within the room, the foundation of the house touching the earth, the earth connected to the neighborhood, the neighborhood within the city, the city within the state, the state within the nation, and the nation touching other nations.

4. *Learn to Listen*

Visit a friend. Allow the friend to converse without any interruption. Allow the entire conversation to be about your friend.

5. *Stamina through Awareness*

Stand up straight with arms folded over chest, relax, and be aware of your feet touching the ground. You may be able to stand for hours by staying aware of your feet touching the ground.

6. *Hands-Movement-Awareness Experience*

While sitting, close your eyes, raise both hands chest high, and slowly turn them with full awareness of each movement.

7. *Personal Sense of I, Me, My, or Mine*

For half a day, do not use the words *I, me, my,* or *mine* in speech or writing. If not half a day, do not use the words for an hour or whatever is possible.

8. *In the Present*

Start a day without any plans. Do only what is given to you to do each moment. Do not plan your next moment—there is none. Stay only in the present moment.

9. *Mind: Resting*

Talk less and listen more. Practice talking when it is only absolutely necessary. Be aware of your thoughts having to rise less often when you talk less. Idle talk helps create a restless mind.

10. Not Distinguishable

The next time anyone praises you, consider it criticism; and the next time anyone criticizes you, consider it praise. Eventually praise and blame are the same.

11. Awakening

When first awakening in the morning, note the first instant of awareness before you are conscious. Note the sequence: awareness, consciousness, mind, and its contents. In that first instant of awareness, there is no content.

12. Present, Past, Future

Imagine you are on a street corner watching a parade approaching. You can see and are aware of its beginnings (present). Imagine you are on a second-story floor watching the same parade. You are able to see and be aware of the passing (past) and more of the rest of the parade coming (future).

Now imagine you have moved to the roof of the house and can view the entire parade—present, past, and future. All are occurring at the same time, in the present, and you are aware of this.

13. Value (Do this exercise only if you are permitted to use salt and pepper).

Label a salt shaker good and a pepper shaker bad. For lunch use only what is labeled good. Then label the salt shaker bad and the pepper shaker good. At dinnertime use only what is labeled good. What changed the shakers' quality?

14. Timeless Day

When you have a free day, remove your wristwatch, cover all clocks in the house, and live a day without time. If a day is too long, do it for a half day and experience the freedom without time.

15. Sound

Gently cup your hand over your left ear. Listen carefully; you may hear the universal "humming" sound. You may also do it with both ears cupped.

16. Write

Write on a piece of paper, "I am." Now draw a diagonal line through the I. Ponder what you have left.

17. No, Yes

Note how often you said no for a day or for a week. Ask yourself if any no could have been a yes. Would that have changed anything? How does it feel to think about this?

18. Silence

Sit comfortably, eyes closed, and place your attention on listening to hear a phone ring. Enjoy the silence.

19. Jesus

If Jesus were standing before you right now, this moment, what would you do? Do it.

Chart Three: Hearts in Triangle

As applied to the Contemplative Invitation Teaching

Christians have the Sacraments to participate in, scriptures to read, silent and verbal prayers to pray. These actions guide a Christian to the inner chamber of their Being—the Spiritual Center.

As one rests within awareness, the arrows are reversed and a Christian's life is lived from the Spiritual Heart Center enhancing the Scriptures, Prayers, Sacraments, and Service.

Appendix

Scripture
Heart and Prayer References

THESE ARE SCRIPTURE verses referring to the heart and prayer. Search out additional ones for yourself.

Scriptural Heart References

1. **"But the LORD said unto Samuel, Look not on his countenance, or on the height of his stature; because I have refused him: for *the LORD seeth* not as man seeth; for man looketh on the outward appearance, but the LORD looketh on the Heart" (1 Sam. 16:7).**
2. **"Let the words of my mouth, and the meditation of my heart be acceptable in thy sight, O LORD, my strength, and my redeemer" (Ps. 19:14).**
3. **"The meek shall eat and be satisfied: they shall praise the LORD that seek him: your heart shall live for ever" (Ps. 22:26).**
4. **"Be glad in the LORD, and rejoice, ye righteous: and shout for joy, all *ye that are* upright in heart" (Ps. 32:11).**

5. "I call to remembrance my song in the night I commune with mine own heart: and my spirit made diligent search" (Ps. 77:6).
6. "I will praise thee, O Lord my God, with all my heart: and I will glorify thy name for evermore" (Ps. 86:12).
7. "Blessed *are* the pure in heart: for they shall see God" (Matt. 6:21).
8. "For where your treasure is, there will your heart be also" (Matt. 6:21).
9. "This people draweth nigh unto me with their mouth, and honoreth me with *their* lips; but their heart is far from me" (Matt. 15:8).
10. "Jesus said unto him, Thou shalt love the Lord thy God with all thy heart, and with all thy soul, and with all thy mind. This is the first and great commandment" (Matt. 22:37–38).
11. "For verily I say unto you, That whosoever shall say unto this mountain, Be thou removed, and be thou cast into the sea; and shall not doubt in his heart, but shall believe that those things which he saith shall come to pass; he shall have whatsoever he saith" (Mark 11:23).
12. "And to love him with all the heart, and with all the understanding, and with all the soul, and with all the strength, and to love *his* neighbor as himself, is more than all whole burnt offerings and sacrifices" (Mark 12:33).
13. "And he shall go before him in the spirit and power of Elias, to turn the hearts of the fathers to the

children, and the disobedient to the wisdom of the just; to make ready a people prepared for the Lord" (Luke 1:17).

14. "But Mary kept all these things, and pondered *them* in her heart" (Luke 2:19).
15. "A good man out of the good treasure of his heart bringeth forth that which is good; and an evil man out of the evil treasure of his heart bringeth forth that which is evil: for of the abundance of the heart his mouth speaketh" (Luke 6:45).
16. "But that on the good ground are they, which in an honest and good heart, having heard the word, keep *it*, and bring forth fruit with patience" (Luke 8:15).
17. "Then he said unto them, O fools, and slow of heart to believe all that the prophets have spoken" (Luke 24:25).
18. "And they said one to another, Did not our heart burn within us, while he talked with us by the way, and while he opened to us the scriptures?" (Luke 24:32).
19. "Let not your heart be troubled: ye believe in God, believe also in me" (John 14:1).
20. "And ye now therefore have sorrow: but I will see you again, and your heart shall rejoice and your joy no man taketh from you" (John 16:22).
21. "Who, when he came, and had seen the grace of God, was glad, and exhorted them all, that with purpose of heart they would cleave unto the Lord" (Acts 11:23).
22. "For David speaketh concerning him, I foresaw the

Lord always before my face, for he is on my right hand, that I should not be moved: Therefore did my heart rejoice and my tongue was glad; moreover also my flesh shall rest in hope" (Acts 2:25–26).

23. "And put no difference between us and them, purifying their hearts by faith" (Acts 15:9).
24. "And hope maketh not ashamed; because the love of God is shed abroad in our hearts by the Holy Ghost which is given unto us" (Rom. 5:5).
25. "And he that searcheth the hearts knoweth what *is* the mind of the Spirit, because he maketh intercession for the saints according to *the will of* God" (Rom. 8:27).
26. "For with the heart man believeth unto righteousness; and with the mouth confession is made unto salvation" (Rom. 10:10).
27. "Now he which stablisheth us with you in Christ, and hath anointed us, *is* God; Who hath also sealed us, and given the earnest of the Spirit in our hearts" (2 Cor. 1:21–22).
28. "And because ye are sons, God hath sent forth the Spirit of his Son into your hearts, crying, Abba, Father" (Gal. 4:6).
29. "That Christ may dwell in your hearts by faith; that ye, being rooted and grounded in love, May be able to comprehend with all saints what *is* the breadth, and length, and depth, and height; And to know the love of Christ, which passeth knowledge, that ye might be filled with all the fullness of God" (Eph. 3:17–19).

30. "Speaking to yourselves in psalms and hymns and spiritual songs, singing and making melody in your heart to the Lord" (Eph. 5:19).
31. "And the peace of God, which passeth all understanding, shall keep your hearts and minds through Christ Jesus" (Phil. 4:7).
32. "That their hearts might be comforted, being knit together in love, and unto all riches of the full assurance of understanding, to the acknowledgment of the mystery of God, and of the Father, and of Christ; In whom are hid all the treasures of wisdom and knowledge" (Col. 2:2–3).
33. "And let the peace of God rule in your hearts, to the which also ye are called in one body; and be ye thankful" (Col. 3:15).
34. "Let the word of Christ dwell in you richly in all wisdom; teaching and admonishing one another in psalms and hymns and spiritual songs, singing with grace in your heart to the Lord" (Col. 3:16).
35. "Now the end of the commandment is charity out of a pure heart, and *of* a good conscience, and *of* faith unfeigned: From which some having swerved have turned aside unto vain jangling" (1 Tim. 1:5–6).
36. "For the word of God *is* quick, and powerful, and sharper than any two edged sword, piercing even to the dividing asunder of soul and spirit, and of the joints and marrow, and *is* a discerner of the thoughts and intents of the heart" (Heb. 4:12).
37. "For this *is* the covenant that I will make with the house of Israel after those days, saith the Lord; I

will put my laws into their mind, and write them in their hearts: and I will be to them a God, and they shall be to me a people" (Heb. 8:10).

38. "Draw nigh to God, and he will draw nigh to you. Cleanse *your* hands, *ye* sinners; and purify *your* hearts, *ye* double minded" (James 4:8).
39. "But sanctify the Lord God in your hearts: and *be* ready always to *give* an answer to every man that asketh you a reason of the hope that is in you with meekness and fear" (1 Peter 3:15).

Scriptural Prayer References

1. "For this shall every one that is godly pray unto thee in a time when thou mayest be found: surely in the floods of great waters they shall not come nigh unto him" (Ps. 32:6).
2. "Be still, and know that I *am* God: I will be exalted among the heathen, I will be exalted in the earth" (Psa. 46:10).
3. "O thou that hearest prayer, unto thee shall all flesh come" (Ps. 65:2).
4. "My meditation of him shall be sweet: I will be glad in the LORD" (Ps. 104:34).
5. "But thou, when thou prayest enter into thy closet, and when thou hast shut thy door, pray to thy Father which is in secret; and thy Father which seeth in secret shall reward thee openly" (Matt. 6:6).
6. "And when he; had sent the multitudes away, he went up into a mountain apart to pray: and when

the evening was come, he was there alone" (Matt. 14:23).

7. "And said unto them, It is written, My house shall be called the house of prayer; but ye have made it a den of thieves" (Matt. 21:13).
8. "And all things, whatsoever ye shall ask in prayer, believing, ye shall receive" (Matt. 21:22).
9. "And when he had sent them away, he departed into a mountain to pray" (Mark 6:46).
10. "And he said unto them, When ye pray, say, Our Father which art in heaven, Hallowed be thy name. Thy kingdom come. Thy will be done, as in heaven, so in earth. Give us day by day our daily bread And forgive us our sins; for we also forgive every one that is indebted to us. And lead us not into temptation; but deliver us from evil" (Luke 11:2–4).
11. "And it came to pass in those days, that he went out into a mountain to pray, and continued all night in prayer to God" (Luke 6:12).
12. "And when he was demanded of the Pharisees, when the kingdom of God should come, he answered them and said, The kingdom of God cometh not with observation: Neither shall they say, Lo here! Or, lo there! for, behold, the kingdom of God is within you" (Luke 17:20).
13. "And being in an agony he prayed more earnestly: and his sweat was as it were great drops of blood falling down to the ground. And when he rose up from prayer, and was come to his disciples, he found

them sleeping for sorrow, And said unto the, Why sleep ye? Rise and pray, lest ye enter into temptation" (Luke 22:44–46).

14. "These all continued with one accord in prayer and supplication, with the women, and Mary the mother of Jesus, and with his brethren" (Acts 1:14).
15. "And they continued steadfastly in the apostles' doctrine and fellowship, and in breaking of bread, and in prayers" (Acts 2:42).
16. "And when he looked on him, he was afraid, and said, What is it, Lord? And he said unto him, Thy prayers and thine alms are come up for a memorial before God" (Acts 10:4).
17. "On the morrow, as they went on their journey, and drew nigh unto the city, Peter went up upon the housetop to pray about the sixth hour" (Acts 10:9).
18. "Peter therefore was kept in prison: but prayer was made without ceasing of the church unto God for him" (Acts 12:5).
19. "Likewise the Spirit also helpeth our infirmities: for we know not what we should pray for as we ought: but the Spirit itself maketh intercession for us with groanings which cannot be uttered" (Rom. 8:26).
20. "What is it then? I will pray with the spirit, and I will pray with the understanding also: I will sing with the spirit, and I will sing with the understanding also" (1 Cor. 14:15).
21. "Praying always with all prayer and supplication in the Spirit and watching there unto with all perseverance and supplication for all saints" (Eph. 6:18).

22. **"Be careful for nothing; but in every thing by prayer and supplication with thanksgiving let your requests be made known unto God. (Phil. 4:6).**
23. **"Continue in prayer, and watch in the same with thanksgiving" (Col. 4:2).**
24. **"Pray without ceasing" (1 Thess. 5:17).**

Bibliography

Casey-Martus, Sandra, and Carla Mancari. *The Lessons: How to Understand Spiritual Principles, Spiritual Activities, and Rising Emotions, Volume One.* Tucson: Wheatmark, 2008.

– – –. *Your "Other Heart": The Best-Kept Secret.* Tucson: Wheatmark, 2010.

The Holy Bible, King James Version. London: Syndics of Cambridge University Press.

Mancari, Carla. *A Diet for the Soul: The Minute Method.* Bloomington, IN: WestBow Press, 2011.

– – –. *Eco-You: A Power of One; Improve Your Health, Improve Your Life.* Bloomington, IN: WestBow Press, 2011.

– – –. *The Minute Method: It's Life Changing! Realize Your Full Potential.* Tucson: Wheatmark, 2012.

– – –. *When Jesus Is the Guru: A Wayward Christian Woman's Spiritual Journey.* Tucson: Wheatmark, 2010.

Authors' Biographies

THE REVEREND SANDRA Casey-Martus is an Episcopal priest, author, teacher, and cofounder of the Contemplative Invitation Teaching: Christ Centered Prayer Method. She holds a BS and an MEd from Springfield College, Massachusetts; an MTS from Oblate School of Theology in San Antonio, Texas; and a CITS from the Episcopal Seminary of Southwest in Austin, Texas.

Reverend Sandy is the rector of Saint Stephen's Episcopal Church in Wimberley,Texas. She served as associate rector of All Saints' Episcopal Church by the Sea in Santa Barbara, California; rector of All Saints' Episcopal Church in Corpus Christi, Texas; and associate rector of All Saints' Episcopal Church, Austin, Texas. She was vicar of St. Francis of the Tetons Episcopal Church and director of the Alta Retreat Center in Alta, Wyoming, from 1994 to 2005.

Reverend Sandy was an adjunct faculty member of the Seminary of the Southwest, and she served for many years on Contemplative Outreach's National teaching and retreat service teams.

Reverend Sandy has been practicing various forms of

contemplative prayer for more than forty years. Presently, along with maintaining her parish ministry, Reverend Sandy writes; teaches the Christ Centered Prayer method to individuals, groups, and organizations; and leads Christ Centered Prayer retreats.

Carla Mancari, author, speaker, spiritual guide, and metaphysical teacher, has shared, nationally and internationally, the Christ Centered prayer method. Carla has been practicing contemplation prayer for more than forty-two years.

Carla holds a BA from the University of South Carolina and an MEd from Orangeburg University, South Carolina. She attended Brigham Young University and the American School in Switzerland.

Carla was featured in *Good Housekeeping*, "The Education of Carla Mancari, 1969," which chronicled the year (1967–1968) she attended the all-black South Carolina State College in Orangeburg, South Carolina.

Carla has served as a certified psychologist. For the protection of minorities' rights, she led a class action suit in the US Supreme Court, *Morton v. Mancari*, in 1973. The case continues to be discussed and studied in university law schools as one of the most important minority-law decisions in minority-law case history.

Carla was a guest on *Larry King Show*. She traveled worldwide for many years, studying with Christian, Hindu, and Buddhist masters. Ultimately, Carla's spiritual quest brought her into an ongoing, personal relationship with Jesus Christ.

For more than thirty-five years, Carla has guided individuals and taught the Christ Centered Prayer and the understanding of spiritual principles. She is the cofounder of the Contemplative Invitation Teaching: The Silent Christ Centered Prayer.

Presently, Carla writes, promotes her published books, does radio interviews, lectures, teaches, and assists with Christ Centered Prayer retreats. Her greatest joy is helping individuals realize their full potential. Contact: charmcarla@gmail.com

Books by the Authors

Casey-Martus, Sandra. "Priestly Spiritual Formation with Centering Prayer." Chap. 9 in *Centering Prayer in Daily Life and Ministry*. New York: Continuum Press, 1998.

Casey-Martus, Sandra, and Carla R. Mancari. *Concordance: For the Lessons, Volume One*. New Jersey: Xlibris, 2008.

———. *The Lessons: How to Understand Spiritual Principles, Spiritual Activities, and Rising Emotions, Volume One*. Tucson: Wheatmark, 2008.

———. *Your "Other Heart": The Best-Kept Secret*. Tucson: Wheatmark, 2010.

Mancari, Carla. *A Diet for the Soul: The Minute Method*. Bloomington, IN: WestBow Press, 2011.

———. *Eco-You: A Power of One: Improve Your Health, Improve Your Life*. Bloomington, IN: WestBow Press, 2011.

———. *The Minute Method: It's Life Changing! Realize Your Full Potential*. Tucson: Wheatmark, 2012.

———. *Walking on the Grass: A White Woman in a Black World*. Macon, GA: Mercer University Press, Macon, 2001.

———. *When Jesus Is the Guru: A Wayward Christian's Spiritual Journey*. Tucson: Wheatmark, 2010.

Websites:

christcenteredprayerpractice.com
contemplativeinvitation.com
theminutemethodpractice.com

You are Heaven and Earth
and all things in between.
You are a moment now
seen and unseen.

NOTES

NOTES

NOTES

NOTES

NOTES

NOTES

You are heaven and earth,
and all things in between.
You are a moment now,
seen and unseen.

Made in the USA
xington, KY
August 2017